The Battle of al-Khafji

by Paul W. Westermeyer

In August 1990, Iraqi military forces invaded the neighboring nation of Kuwait. The invasion was part of an expansionist foreign policy that President Saddam Hussein established a decade earlier when he invaded post-revolution Iran. The Iraqi invasion of Iran failed, degenerating into a decade long war of attrition, but Kuwait was an easier target. Kuwait had financed the Iraq-Iran War for Iraq, but refused to forgive the debt, and Iraq accused Kuwait of stealing oil from the Rumalia Oil Field. Much smaller than Iran in terms of population and geography, Kuwait had focused its foreign and defense policies on negotiation and compromise rather than military force; inevitably, the large Iraqi Army quickly overwhelmed the small Kuwaiti armed forces.

Inside Kuwait, Iraqi troops began wholesale pillaging as security forces moved to remove all those loyal to the Kuwaiti royal family. Iraq declared that Kuwait was now a province, thus eliminating its debt and adding extensive oil fields to its own. Saddam stationed conscript infantry divisions in Kuwait and began building extensive defenses along the Kuwaiti-Saudi border.

While Saddam calculated the military balance between Iraq and Kuwait correctly, he underestimated the willingness of the world community, especially the United States and Great Britain, to intervene on Kuwait's behalf. His invasion set the stage for a military confrontation that was larger in scope than any similar circumstance since the Cold War. Under President George H. W. Bush, the United States assembled a global coalition of concerned nations, first to defend Saudi Arabia against further Iraqi aggression, and then to eject the Iraqi military from Kuwait. Early in this "Gulf War" American military commanders designated the operation to protect Saudi Arabia "Desert Shield," and the successive operation to free Kuwait "Desert Storm." These military operations were massive undertakings, and they highlighted the paradigm shift from superpowers in precarious equilibrium during the Cold War to American global hegemony in the 1990s.

The Gulf War would be the largest deployment of Marines since the Vietnam War. It challenged the entire warfighting establishment of the Marine Corps—aviation, ground, and logistics—forcing a generation of Marines to put two decades of planning and training to the test. The Corps would see many of its tactical and operational philosophies justified under combat conditions. The maritime prepositioning ships program, for one, proved its worth, enabling Marines to be the first combined arms task force in Saudi Arabia. In addition, Marines tested the air-ground task force concept within the joint environment.

Marines of the 7th Marine Expeditionary Brigade arrived in Saudi Arabia in late August, where they married up with their equipment from the maritime prepositioning ships. Under Marine Forces Commander, Central Command, and Commander, I Marine Expeditionary Force, Lieutenant General Walter E. Boomer, Marines continued to deploy to the Gulf and solidify the defenses of Saudi Arabia. They trained, established defensive positions, and watched the diplomatic efforts attempt to resolve the crisis.

As fall turned to winter, the Marine Corps continued the massive logistical enterprise, deploying personnel and equipment of I Marine Expeditionary Force: 1st and 2d Marine Divisions, 3d Marine Aircraft Wing, and the 1st Force Service Support Group.

General H. Norman Schwarzkopf, the United States Central Command commander, chose the Marines to evict the Iraqis from Kuwait proper, fighting alongside Arab members of the Coalition. As Lieutenant General Boomer's I Marine Expeditionary Force and its partners prepared to breach the fortifications separating Kuwait from Saudi Arabia, the 4th and 5th Marine Expeditionary Brigades remained afloat in the Persian Gulf onboard the ships of U.S. Navy amphibious ready groups, providing a seaborne threat which would eventually tie up many Iraqi resources along the shoreline.

Despite the threat of a Coalition military intervention, Iraq refused to withdraw from Kuwait. Saddam was convinced that the United States could neither maintain the Coalition, nor intervene militarily in a meaningful way. A military struggle to free Kuwait thus became inevitable.

The Air Campaign[1]

On 17 January 1991, Operation Desert Storm began with massive air strikes throughout Iraq and Kuwait. Although the operation had an expected ground component, U.S. Air Force strategists, who believed that bombing alone could compel Iraq to relinquish Kuwait, drove the first phases. As a result, the primary focus of the campaign was on achieving air superiority (accomplished the first evening), striking strategic targets inside Iraq, then annihilating Iraq's elite *Republican Guard* centered in southern Iraqi, and finally hitting Iraqi forces in Kuwait proper.

During the air campaign, Marine aviation conducted hundreds of sorties

On The Cover: The crew of a Marine LAV-25 scans the desert. The LAV-25 was the backbone of the light armored infantry battalions, an untried concept prior to the Battle of al-Khafji. The battalions were used in a traditional cavalry role, providing a screen in front of the main body of I Marine Expeditionary Force.
History Division Photo

At Left: *A Qatari AMX-30 tank leads two Saudi V-150 Commando armored cars, the first of which is an antitank variant, into al-Khafji through the town arches. The arches were the focal point of each Saudi counterattack into the city.* Used with permission of Jody Harmon
(www.jodyharmon.com)

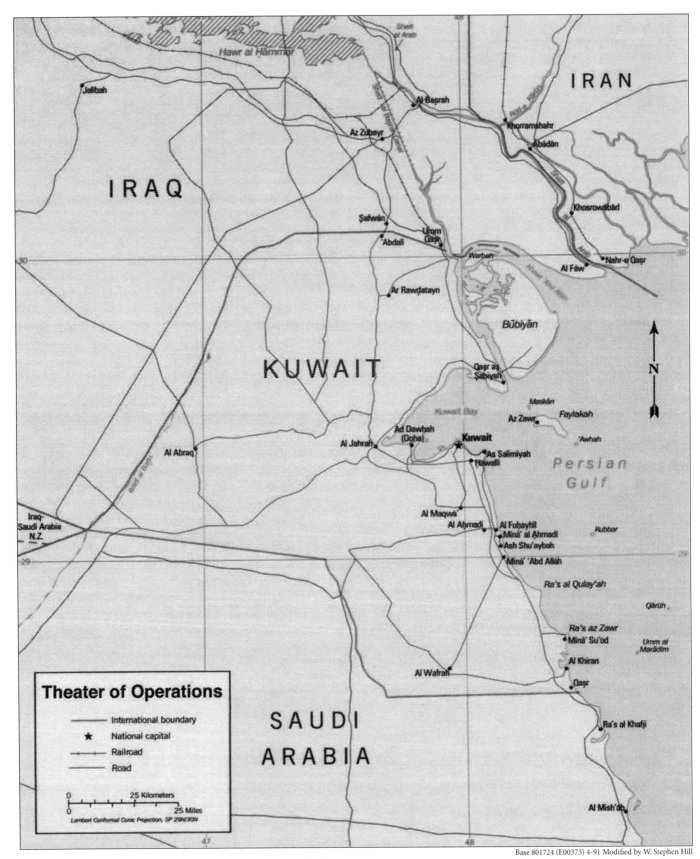

against enemy positions in Kuwait and Iraq. Aircrews of the 3d Marine Aircraft Wing struck Iraqi command and control centers, antiaircraft defenses, and strategic targets deep inside Iraq, and later performed traditional reconnaissance, battlefield interdiction, and close air support missions in Kuwait.

A day after the air campaign began, a distraction was added when Iraq began firing SS-1 Scud-B Al Hussein surface-to-surface medium range missiles against Israel and Saudi Arabia. The political and military consequences of the Scud attacks forced Central Command to immediately instigate the "Great Scud Hunt." Although the hunt was unsuccessful, it diverted large numbers of aircraft and reconnaissance resources away from Kuwait and into the western Iraqi desert. In particular, the hunt required the use of the two prototype Northrup Grumman E-8C joint surveillance and target acquisition radar system (JSTARS) aircraft. The E-8C aircraft had arrived in Saudi Arabia after Christmas and was a new, untested battlefield technology.[2] Central Command used the planes to track mobile Scud launchers in the western desert, although originally designed to track large-scale troop movements, like those that would precede a major offensive.[3]

Despite the Scud distraction and the focus on strategic rather than operational targets, the air campaign had an obvious and significant impact on Iraqi forces inside Kuwait. It isolated units from the national command authority, degraded troop morale, and made even simple movements difficult, often requiring days of detailed planning.

With its diplomatic options exhausted, and enduring the effects of an air campaign much longer than anticipated, Iraq launched a large spoiling attack centered on the Saudi town of al-Khafji on 29 January 1991. Now known as the "Battle of al-Khafji," it was the first major ground combat action of the Gulf War.

Iraq's Plan[4]

Saddam Hussein was prepared for a confrontation with the United States prior to the invasion of Kuwait, as evidenced by his comments to Palestinian leader Yasser Arafat in April 1990:

> We are ready for it. We will fight America, and, with God's will, we will defeat it and kick it out of the whole region. Because it is not about the fight itself; we know that America has a larger air force than us… has more rockets than us, but I think that when the Arab people see real action of war, when it is real and not only talk, they will fight America everywhere. So we have to get ready to fight America; we are ready to fight when they do; when they strike, we strike.[5]

But Iraq's president was convinced the

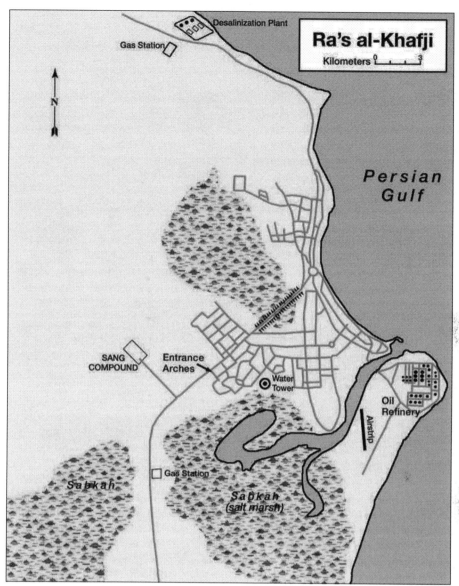

Map by W. Stephen Hill

United States would not fight, in part because of the muted response to the Iraqi Aérospatiale AM39 Exocet antiship missile attack on the USS *Stark* (FFG 31) in 1987. The massive military buildup in Saudi Arabia throughout the fall of 1990 did not change his mind. Moreover, he believed that even if the United States desired a military confrontation, the Soviet Union would intervene to prevent it.

If an attack did occur, Saddam was equally convinced that his massive military could inflict sufficient losses on the Americans to force them to abandon the struggle. He considered the American withdrawal from Vietnam indicative of America's lack of resolve. The United States suffered 58,000 dead in the Vietnam War; in comparison Iraq had lost 51,000 in a single battle with the Iranians on the al-Faw Peninsula in 1986.[6] He believed then, as he stated after the war, "America is not in the prime of youth. America is in the last stage of elderliness and the beginning of the first stage of old age."[7]

Iraq had survived the long, 10-year slaughter of the "Khadisya Saddam," as the Iraqis termed the Iran-Iraq War, and Saddam believed that the conflict over Kuwait, if it came to blows, would follow a similar pattern.[8] Air power would be relatively ineffective; the main conflict would be a set piece battle as American forces impotently tried to breach the defenses built along the Kuwaiti-Saudi border. American losses would be severe, the American people would demand an end to the bloodshed, and the American government would then negotiate a peace. In the aftermath, Iraq would become the undisputed regional power, while American, and Western, influence in the Middle East would suffer a near fatal blow.

Events did not follow Saddam Hussein's expectations. The United States was determined not to allow the Iraqi aggression to stand and Iraq's Arab neighbors recognized the degree to which Iraq's invasion of Kuwait would upset the regional balance of power. The Soviet Union was unwilling and unable to support Iraq in an aggressive adventure that offered no tangible benefits. The United States was able to form an international coalition that included an impressive variety of nations; notable members included Great Britain, France, Saudi Arabia, Egypt, and Syria. Despite its variety, the Coalition's unity was never seriously challenged by Iraqi attempts to fracture it.

The United States and its allies began the war with the air strikes Saddam and his generals had predicted, but these attacks were far more effective than expected. Later, Iraqis would master the art of proofing their country against aerial attack, but in January 1991, the Coalition air campaign was something the Iraqis had never experienced.

Saddam responded quickly with Scud missile attacks on Saudi Arabia and Israel, and while these strikes were unquestionably the most effective military and political tactic employed by Iraq during the conflict, they did not end the raids, noticeably decrease their severity, spur the United States into a premature ground assault, nor bring Israel into the war and thus splinter the multinational Coalition which Iraq faced.

In addition to the Scud attacks, Iraq tried to provoke Coalition ground operations by setting Kuwaiti oil fields afire and by creating a large oil slick in the Persian Gulf that threatened Saudi water desalination facilities. But these actions were no more effective than the Scud attacks.

Saddam expected the air campaign to last a week, and then be followed by the ground war, the "Mother of All Wars," which would produce the desired massive American casualties. Instead, the bombing showed no sign of stopping, and was inflicting serious damage on the Iraqi forces without any corresponding ability to produce the desired Coalition casualties. Something needed to be done in order to goad the United States into the planned Kuwaiti "meat-grinder."

An Iraqi War College study, completed later, highlighted the Iraqi understanding of the situation in late January 1991:

In military practice, there are principles. One of the important principles is that the attack is the best defense. In the Mother of Wars this principle is particularly important, because the enemy of Iraq and the Arab nation has deployed a large number of airplanes, rockets and modern equipment, from which it seems they are prepared for a total war. They deployed the most modern equipment for their field forces, which consist of the armies of 28 nations totaling half a million men. But for all this great power, they hesitate to attack the Iraqi field forces because they realize how well the Iraqi forces can defend against a ground attack. And, they know already, the military genius of Iraq's leader, Saddam Hussein.[9]

The Iraqis believed they understood American intentions: "Like we say, they intend to destroy our forces and the infrastructure of our country through the air attack, by airplanes and long range missiles. And they want to avoid the losses of a ground war as much as they can."[10] Moreover, "George Bush will not be able to handle the heavy responsibility of heavy casualties in front of Congress and public opinion."[11] In this case, the Iraqis did understand American intentions, although they underestimated American resolve, and gravely overestimated the ability of the Iraqi military to inflict losses on the attacking Coalition forces.

The al-Khafji operation was intended to spark the ground battle of the "Mother of Wars" which Saddam felt was the prerequisite for his eventual victory. It was intended as a provoking raid that would draw the Americans into a hasty and massive military response and result in significant American casualties. Despite his deficient military acumen, he correctly identified that the center of gravity in the Coalition war effort was the willingness of the American people to suffer casualties, and he designed his operational plans to strike directly at that willpower.

President Saddam chose al-Khafji as the target of the attack for several reasons. The Iraqi War College analysis noted that it had two harbors: one designed specifically for exporting oil, and the other the Iraqis believed was a base for Coalition forces. An Iraqi force occupying the town would be able to threaten Coalition naval forces in the Gulf. Al-Khafji was also within range of Iraqi supporting artillery in Kuwait. The attack also would force

The arches into the Saudi city of al-Khafji proclaim that "The municipality and residents of Khafji welcome the honorable visitor." Because the city was within range of Iraqi artillery in Kuwait, it was ordered evacuated on 18 August 1990.

Photo courtesy of MGySgt Gregory L. Gillispie

the Saudis to respond; he knew they could not permit him to hold any part of their kingdom for long. It seemed likely that the attack would force the Coalition into the bloody ground war Saddam wanted.[12]

The operational plan for implementing Iraq's strategic goal was relatively straight forward. Five Iraqi infantry divisions defended the Saudi-Kuwaiti border from the coast to the "elbow": from east to west, they were the *18th Infantry, 8th Infantry, 29th Infantry, 14th Infantry,* and *7th Infantry Divisions.* These commands would not take part in the offensive, instead they would continue to defend the fortifications along the border. These border fortifications, called the "Saddam Line" by U.S. forces, consisted of a belt of minefields, antitank obstacles, and triangular brigade strong points. Iraqi engineers had designed and constructed the belt based on lessons learned in their 10-year war with Iran.

The attacking forces would be drawn from the *3d Armored* and *5th Mechanized Divisions* of *III Corps,* under Major General Salah Aboud Mahmoud, and the *1st Mechanized Division* of *IV Corps* under Major General Yaiyd Khalel Zaki. Major General Salah Aboud had over all command of the operation; *III Corps,* considered one of the better organizations in the Iraqi Army, had successfully conducted similar operations during the Iran-Iraq War, as well as performing successfully while defending the Iraqi city of Basrah.[13]

The armored battalions of these divisions were equipped with a combination of T-54/55 and T-62 main battle tanks while their mechanized infantry battalions were equipped with BMP-1 armored personnel carriers supported by BRDM-2 scout vehicles. Their divisional artillery was lavishly equipped with various models of 152mm and 155mm howitzers.[14]

The plan called for the *1st Mechanized Division* to pass through the lines of the *7th* and *14th Infantry Divisions* between the border's "heel" just south of Umm Hajul and the "elbow" at al-Manaqish (see map on page 12). This maneuver was intended to protect the flank of Brigadier General Hussan Zedin's *3d Armored Division* as it traversed the al-Wafrah oil fields and the lines of the *8th* and *29th Infantry Divisions.* The *3d Armored Division* would then take up a blocking position to the west of al-Khafji. Al-

Khafji itself was the target of the *5th Mechanized Division,* which was to seize and fortify the town. Once the *5th Mechanized Division* had secured al-Khafji, the *1st Mechanized* and *3d Armored Divisions* would withdraw back into Kuwait. In theory, after the Coalition ground response was provoked, the *5th Mechanized Division* would retire from al-Khafji and move safely behind the massive fortifications along the Saudi-Kuwait border.[15] The attack was set to be launched at 2000 on 29 January 1991, and al-Khafji was to be occupied by 0100 on 30 January 1991.

General Salah Aboud ordered that the forces be "dug in" and "hidden underground" by the morning of 30 January. He provided some insightful tactical advice as well: "I emphasized the use, and the importance of shoulder fired anti-aircraft weapons in ambush in the front and flanks of the fortified positions. And I emphasized how the snipers should be active and effective against the helicopters of the enemy." He instructed his men to light tire fires, as the smoke would confuse the infrared sensors of the Coalition forces. Finally, he ordered his troops "to be economic with the ammunition which is in the tanks and the carriers. Because the enemy air will be focused on the battle territory, especially the transportation, so movement will be very limited."[16] Whatever Saddam's understanding of the battle, at least one of his generals anticipated the difficulties the Iraqis would face trying to maneuver against overwhelming Coalition air superiority.

The capture of American personnel was a high priority. Saddam had deter-

Iraqi Armored Vehicles

Vehicle	Type	Armament	Top Speed
	T-54/55	100mm main gun 1300m effective range Coax 7.62mm MG Bow 7.62mm MG 12.7mm MG	50kph
	T-62	115mm main gun 2000m effective range Coax 7.62mm MG Bow 7.62mm MG 12.7mm MG	50kph
	BMP-1	73mm smoothbore cannon 7.62mm MG AT-3 Sagger ATGM 8 troops	80kph
	BRDM-2	14.5mm MG 7.62mm MG 4 troops	100kph

The Battle of al-Khafji

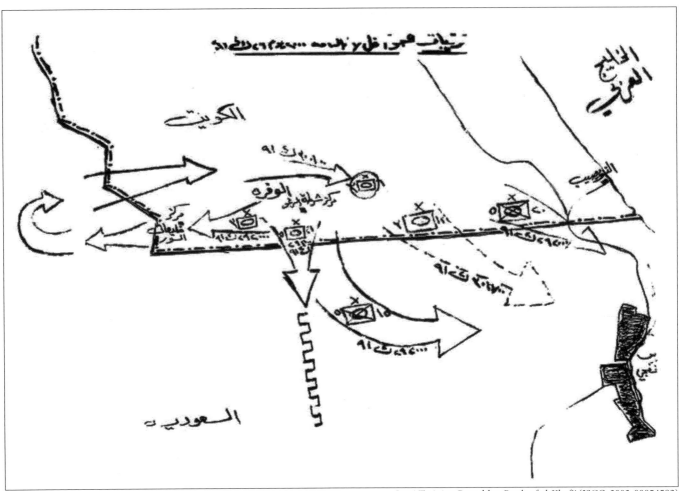

Iraqi Training Pamphlet, Battle of al-Khafji (ISGQ-2003-00054592)

Part of the Iraqi plan for the Battle of al-Khafji, as shown in an official Iraqi history of the battle. This sketch indicates that 6th Armored Brigade's attack on Observation Post 4 was not intended as the main Iraqi effort.

mined from the American prisoner of war experience during the Vietnam War and the Iranian hostage crisis that the United States was vulnerable to hostage taking. He held many Westerners hostage early in the crisis, but released them in December 1990 with little obvious advantage. He felt, however, that American soldiers would still be excellent bargaining chips in the confrontation. An Iraqi prisoner from the battle later told American interrogators: "The sole purpose of the raid on al-Khafji was to capture Coalition personnel. The loss of all Iraqi equipment and personnel involved in the raid was of no importance as long as POWs were captured."[17]

When giving orders for the attack to his corps commanders, Saddam summed up Iraqi goals: the "enemy in front of us, if he faces this time our willingness to cause severe damage to him, he won't be able to handle it. He will be destroyed and the news will be heard. And all the chairs of the enemy governments will shake."[18] For Iraq, the Battle of al-Khafji was not intended as a skirmish; it was intended to win the war by destroying the Coalition's will to fight. At the heart of the Coalition was the alliance between the United States and Saudi Arabia.

American and Saudi Arabian Relations

The United States began providing the Kingdom of Saudi Arabia with military assistance in the 1940s, and as the decades passed the relationship grew. The United States assisted the kingdom as a bulwark first against communism and secular ethnic Arab nationalist movements, and later against radical Islamic movements. In addition, a strong, stable Saudi Arabia was seen as the key to preventing a general war in the Middle East. For the House of Saud, the close relationship and military assistance of the United States acted as a counter to Saudi Arabia's more powerful neighbors Iraq and Egypt, as well as aiding in the suppression of internal rebellious movements.[19]

As the decades passed, however, and hostility against the United States increased in the broader Islamic world, American military assistance became nearly as much of a liability as it was an asset. This paradox was neatly summarized by leading Egyptian journalist, Mohamed Heikal: "the first responsibility of a Saudi monarch is to keep intimate relations with Washington, and the second is to do all he can to hide it."[20]

The Iraqi invasion of Kuwait produced a near catastrophe in foreign relations for the Saudis, as it was clear they could not stop any Iraqi encroachment into their territory without American aid, yet that aid would have to be very public. The intimate relationship between the United States and Saudi Arabia had long been an open secret, but now it would truly be exposed. The presence of a massive "infidel" army on Saudi soil, home to Mecca and Medina, the two holiest cities in Islam (forbidden to nonbelievers), was a potential public relations disaster. On the other hand, Saddam had invaded Kuwait, a fellow Arab country that had materially aided Iraq in its war against Iran. Moreover, Saddam's own Ba'athist party was an avowedly secular organization devoted in part to ethnic Arab nationalism. Both of these facts helped Saudi Arabia maintain its image in the Islamic world while accepting American aid. But the situation required constant, careful manipulation. There were many tensions between the Saudis, who naturally wished Coalition forces would disrupt Saudi life as little as possible, and the Coalition forces who often felt unappreciated by the Saudis they were ostensibly in the desert to protect.

Saudi military forces were divided into two distinct services. The Ministry of Defense and Aviation (MODA) consisted of the regular Saudi ground and aviation forces, whose mission was to protect the kingdom from external threats. The

Gen Khaled bin Sultan bin Saud, a prince of the Saudi royal family, was the Joint Forces Commander and General Schwartzkopf's opposite number. Joint Forces Command was composed of the Coalition's Islamic members forces: Saudi Arabia, Egypt, Syria, and others. The Battle of al-Khafji was the first conflict on Saudi soil in decades; as a result Gen Khaled was pressured to end the battle decisively and quickly.

DVIC DA-ST-92-08034

Saudi aviation forces were folded, along with other Coalition air forces, into the air campaign, but the Royal Saudi Land Forces or Saudi Army operated separately as nine brigades.[21]

The Ministry of Defense and Aviation units were supplemented by the Saudi Arabian National Guard (SANG) comprised of two mechanized brigades. Ostensibly the Saudi Arabian National Guard was intended to reinforce the Ministry of Defense and Aviation forces in the event of a war, but in reality the Saudi National Guard's primary role was to protect the royal family from internal rebellion. Staffed with personnel loyal to the House of Saud specifically through family and tribal ties, the Saudi Arabian National Guard was descended from the Ikhwan (White Army), a Wahhabi tribal militia, which formed the main body of Ibn Saud's forces during World War I. The Saudi government employed the National Guard to protect the holy cities of Mecca and Medina, and to counter the regular armed forces in the event of an attempted coup. It received the lion's share of training and equipment that was available to Saudi forces, although it did not possess tanks.[22]

The Saudi National Guard was favored over the Ministry of Aviation and Defense. The Royal family kept the two forces separated, and neither force trained with the other. Nevertheless, oil-rich Saudi Arabia did not lack resources and both services were lavishly equipped with modern military hardware. Despite massive amounts spent on modernization, many Saudi soldiers lacked professional standards or competence and the officer corps granted the noncommissioned officers neither authority nor responsibility.

In 1990-1991, direct American military assistance to Saudi Arabia centered around two organizations. Officially, there was the Department of Defense's Office of Program Manager for the Modernization of the Saudi National Guard, which assigned American officers as advisors to the Saudi National Guard. In addition, the Vinnell Corporation provided military contract advisors to the Saudi National Guard, most of whom were American veterans of the Vietnam War. In both cases, the personnel assigned to train the Saudi National Guard prior to the invasion of Kuwait fought with the National Guard forces, greatly increasing their effectiveness. The military advisors and Vinnell Corporation employees worked closely together supporting the Saudi National Guard.[23]

Since neither Saudi Arabia nor the United States was willing to have its forces under the other's command, a joint structure was set up. Joint Forces Command, a parallel organization of Central Command, was composed of most of the Arab contingents and was led by Saudi General Khaled bin Sultan. A nephew of King Fahd, he was a graduate of the Royal Military Academy, Sandhurst, and the Air War College at Maxwell Air Force Base, Alabama. In 1986, after 25 years in the armed forces of his country, General Khaled was appointed commander of the Royal Saudi Air Defence Forces.

The command was further subdivided into Joint Forces Command-North and Joint Forces Command-East. Joint Forces Command-North, although dominated by two Egyptian divisions, also contained Saudi Arabian Ministry of Defense and Aviation, Kuwaiti, and Syrian brigades. It controlled the territory from the "elbow" at al-Manaqish to the Kuwait-Iraq border. Saudi National Guard units, Ministry of Defense and Aviation forces, as well as Kuwaiti forces and a Qatari mechanized brigade made up Joint Forces Command-East. It controlled the territory from the eastern border of the al-Wafrah oil fields to the Persian Gulf coast, including al-Khafji and the surrounding territory.[24] The assignment of National Guard units under the command of General Khaled was out of the ordinary, and indicated how seriously the House of Saud took the crisis.[25] The placement of the subcommands was due to Arab pride which dictated that they hold positions in the front line to ensure theirs would be the first blood shed.

Although well equipped, and provided with professional military advisors, the Saudi forces were still not up to Western military standards. Islamic holidays, daily prayers, and familial obligations dramatically decreased the amount of training. The troops generally averaged an eighth grade education. The officers were often well educated and most spoke at least some English, but they were discouraged from independent thought or action until given battalion-level command. They faced tremendous pressure to keep their superiors happy. As Captain Joseph Molofsky, 3d Marines liaison officer to the 2d Brigade of the Saudi Arabian National Guard, noted: "It's all make or break. You displease your senior and you're done forever. You make him happy and he sends you on vacation to Europe. Literally."[26] Saudi forces were untested in 1991, having last seen action in the 1920s. There was serious concern about how well they would perform in battle.[27]

As Desert Shield progressed, additional liaison elements were attached to the Saudi forces. United States Army Special Forces teams were attached to Ministry of Defense and Aviation forces at the brigade level, and the Marine Corps assigned 1st Air-Naval Gunfire Liaison Company (1st ANGLICO) teams throughout Joint Forces Command-East.[28] When it became clear that the 1st Marine Division would be fighting beside Saudi forces, the division's commander, Major General James M. Myatt, ordered

his assistant division commander, Brigadier General Thomas V. Draude, to take primary responsibility for liaison duties.[29] Brigadier General Draude used 3d Marines, the Marine unit nearest to Joint Forces Command-East units, as the primary focus of his liaison effort. As Colonel John A. Admire, commander of the 3d Marines, noted:

We were the only U.S. combat force located on the eastern coast. Now the significance of that of course is that we continued to train with Coalition forces. We were the division's primary instrument from October-November-December and through January of training with the Saudis and training with the Qatari forces.

Colonel Admire assigned Captain Molofsky, an officer with previous experience in the Middle East serving with the United Nations on the Sinai Peninsula, as the 3d Marines liaison officer to the 2d Brigade, Saudi Arabian National Guard.[30] From the beginning, there was tension between the Marines and the Saudis. "The Marines felt that they needed to get their own eyes on," Captain Molofsky explained. "They couldn't trust the Saudis. The Saudis were insulted that the Marines didn't trust them."[31] This situation was exacerbated in January 1991 when 3d Marines was given the duty of protecting the town and airfield of al-Mishab. Previously al-Mishab had been part of Joint Force Command-East's area of operations; placing it within the Marine area of operations, especially as the United States began to use the airfield, implied a lack of faith in Saudi military capabilities on the part of Marine commanders.[32]

In addition to the U.S. Army advisors and Special Forces teams assigned to the Saudi forces, commanders attached air-naval gunfire liaison teams to coordinate Marine air and artillery support for the Saudis. Specifically, 1st ANGLICO was attached to Joint Forces Command-East, and in turn the company assigned supporting arms liaison teams to Saudi brigades and fire control teams to Saudi battalions. These teams worked closely with their Saudi counterparts, developing excellent working relationships.[33]

On the eve of the battle of al-Khafji,

Coalition Armored Vehicles

Vehicle	Type	Armament	Top Speed
	AMX-30	105mm main gun Coax 12.7mm MG 7.62mm MG	65kph
	M-60	105mm main gun Coax 7.62mm MG 12.7mm MG	48kph
	LAV-25	25mm main gun 2 x 7.62mm MG 4 troops or TOW-2 ATGM	100kph
	V-150	.50 caliber MG 6-8 troops or 4 troops TOW-2 ATGM	88kph
	M-113	12.7mm MG 11 troops or 4 troops TOW ATGM	61kph

American and Saudi forces had worked and trained together for five months. There was some unease between the two forces, but both sides had made a concerted effort to overcome it. The Iraqi invasion would put those efforts to the test.

Ra's al-Khafji

The Saudi coastal town of Ra's al-Khafji, more commonly know as al-Khafji, lies approximately seven miles south of the Saudi-Kuwait border. Before the war, the primary industries in the town were oil and tourism, but it was essentially deserted just prior to the attack. General Khaled bin Sultan had ordered the town evacuated in August because it was too close to the Kuwaiti border to properly defend.[34] North of the town there was a water desalination plant, and to the south there was an oil refinery, a pier, and a small airstrip. Southeast, beyond the town's outskirts, was a Saudi Arabian National Guard compound.

Ra's al-Khafji was particularly difficult to defend because the town lies to the north of extensive *sabkhas* or salt marshes. As Captain Molofsky explained: "A *sabkha* is a patch of desert that has some kind of underlying moisture that causes a thin, mud like crust to develop on the top, which cracks in the heat, but it's easily penetrated by a vehicle and very soft underneath—you get stuck in it in a huge way."[35] The *sabkhas* served to chan-

Photo courtesy of Capt Charles G. Grow

Saudi soldiers move through the evacuated border city of al-Khafji. Although the city's architecture was relatively monotonous it offered civilized amenities and was a popular stop for Coalition commanders and journalists.

nel traffic onto the coastal highway, especially the heavy vehicles needed to support the logistics of large military forces.

Coalition Dispositions

Covering deployed Coalition forces were a series of observation posts strung out along the Kuwaiti-Saudi border. Each post was situated near a Saudi border fort, described by virtually every eyewitness as a "*Beau Geste* fort." U.S. Navy Sea, Air, and Land (SEAL), Army Special Forces, and Marine reconnaissance teams manned these posts in order to gather intelligence on Iraqi forces in Kuwait. Placed at 10 to 20 kilometer intervals, Observation Post 8 was set on the coast, Observation Post 7, further to the west, with Observation Posts 2, 1, 4, 5, and 6 following the border until the "elbow" was reached at al-Jathathil.*

Nearest to the coast, the Marine Corps' 1st Surveillance, Reconnaissance, and Intelligence Group controlled Observation Posts 8, 7, and 2.** The coastal highway ran between Observation Post 7 and Observation Post 8, which gave those two posts overlapping oversight of the most likely route into al-Khafji. In addition to the special operations teams, air-naval gunfire supporting arms liaison teams also occupied these observation posts. The 1st Surveillance, Reconnaissance, and

The crew of a Marine LAV-25 scans the desert. The LAV-25 was the backbone of the light armored infantry battalions, an untried concept prior to the Battle of al-Khafji. The battalions were used in a traditional cavalry role, providing a screen in front of the main body of I Marine Expeditionary Force.

History Division Photo

---
*Most works on the Battle of al-Khafji list the observation posts slightly differently from east to west: OP-8, OP-7, OP-1, OP-2, OP-4, OP-5, and OP-6. Two important primary sources, the command chronology of the 2d Light Armored Infantry Battalion and the after action report of 1st ANGLICO/1st Surveillance, Reconnaissance, and Intelligence Group both make clear that the order should be the one given in the text.

**The 1st Surveillance, Reconnaissance, and Intelligence Group (1st SRIG) was a unit responsible for coordinating intelligence gathering operations, and was subordinate to the I Marine Expeditionary Force (I MEF) rather than the 1st Marine Division. Its primary headquarters was with the I MEF headquarters, but it maintained a forward headquarters in al-Khafji.

Intelligence Group had a headquarters at the desalination plant located to the north of al-Khafji.[36] The 1st Air-Naval Gunfire Liaison Company, attached to Joint Forces Command-East, was a subordinate unit of the 1st Surveillance, Reconnaissance, and Intelligence Group, which coordinated closely in and around al-Khafji with the various units in the Kuwaiti border area.

Task Force Shepherd (1st Light Armored Infantry Battalion) of the 1st Marine Division had companies on a screening mission near Observation Post 4 (Company D), Observation Post 5 (Company B) and Observation Post 6 (Company C). Only Observation Post 4 had a Marine reconnaissance platoon in place when the Iraqi attack occurred on 29 January.[37]* The 2d Marine Division's 2d Light Armored Infantry Battalion established a similar screen to the east directly in front of the al-Wafrah oil fields and Observation Post 1, between Task Force Shepherd and the Joint Forces Command-East area of operations along the coast.

Under the command of Major General Sultan 'Adi al-Mutairi, Joint Forces Command-East was further divided into task forces. Abu Bakr Task Force, comprised of the 2d Saudi Arabian National Guard Brigade and an attached Qatari armored battalion, was responsible for al-Khafji and the surrounding desert. The 2d Saudi Arabian National Guard Brigade's 5th Battalion established a screen north of al-Khafji and west of the coastal highway, behind Observation Post 7. Tariq Task Force, comprised of the nascent Saudi Arabian Marines as well as a battalion of Moroccan infantry, was along the coast south of al-Khafji. Further west was Othman Task Force, built around the 8th Mechanized Ministry of Defense and Aviation Brigade. A battalion of the 8th Brigade served as a screening force behind Observation Posts 2 and 7. In addition, further west in Joint Forces Command-East's area of operation was Omar Task Force, built around the 10th Mechanized Ministry of Defense and Avi-

---

* The 1st Marine Division's 1st Light Armored Infantry Battalion was actually a composite organization with companies from three separate light armored infantry battalions. To encourage a sense of identity in the ad hoc battalion, it was designated Task Force Shepherd.

ation Brigade, with a battalion serving as a screen behind the border. The Saudi mechanized screens were approximately three kilometers behind the border, while the main Saudi defensive positions were approximately 20 kilometers behind the screen.[38]

The I Marine Expeditionary Force's area of operations at this time was shaped somewhat like a fat "L." The leg of the "L" extended along the bend of the Saudi-Kuwaiti border from al-Jathathil to just east of the oil fields at al-Wafrah and the foot of the "L" extended south of Joint Forces Command-East's area of operations to al-Mishab and the airfield. Al-Mishab and the surrounding area were held by Task Force Taro, built around the 3d Marines. The pillar of the "L" was held by Task Force Shepherd and 2d Light Armored Infantry Battalion, which stretched along the border in a light armored screen. Behind this screen was the massive Marine logistical base at Kibrit, which Lieutenant General Boomer, commander of I Marine Expeditionary Force, decided to place forward of the main Marine combat forces, in order to speed the eventual attack into Kuwait. Kibrit was relatively vulnerable, and during the Iraqi attack on al-Khafji, Brigadier General Charles C. Krulak, commander of the Direct Support Command and the Kibrit logistics base, would quickly call for armored forces to establish positions north of the base. There is little indication, however, that the Iraqis were ever aware of the base, or its importance to future Marine operations in the region.[39]

Colonel Admire, responsible for the defense of al-Mishab, was unconvinced that Saudi forces between the Marines and the Iraqis would fight if attacked. In January, he began to run reconnaissance training missions into the town of al-Khafji. Teams from the 3d Platoon, Company A, 3d Reconnaissance Battalion, then attached to Task Force Taro, would infiltrate the city by vehicle, usually humvees, establish an observation post, and then leave a day or so later. Unfortunately, these missions were not coordinated with the Coalition forces in al-Khafji. This would have a dramatic impact during the Iraqi invasion, as Captain Molofsky later noted: "I was unaware, [1st ANGLICO's Captain James R.] Braden was unaware, and the Saudis were un-

aware, that the Marines had reconnaissance teams up in al-Khafji."[40]

Other Marine operations would lead to the Coalition's success at al-Khafji, however. In response to the difficulties involved in defending Saudi Arabia from an Iraqi attack in the early days of Operation Desert Shield, Marine planners had developed Task Force Cunningham. They designed it as a task organized, aviation only task force that would stop Iraqi ground maneuver forces with concentrated fire from the air, covering the withdrawal of Saudi and Marine forces along the coastal highway. Bell UH-1N Huey and AH-1W Super Cobra helicopters would operate alongside North American OV-10D Broncos and McDonnell Douglas AV-8B Harrier II fixed wing aircraft in the task force. Joint Forces Command-East liked the plan, and it would serve as the model for air support during the battle.[41]

Artillery Raids

After the air campaign against Iraq began, I Marine Expeditionary Force began a series of artillery raids against Iraqi forces in Kuwait. The first artillery raid occurred on the night of 21 January, and was fired from a location just north of al-Khafji against enemy artillery positions north of the border. Two subsequent raids occurred on the nights of 26 January and 28 January. The 26 January raid was near the "elbow" at al-Jathathil, while the third was again from just north of al-Khafji. Although Iraqi counter-battery fire was ineffective, there was a vehicular accident during the 26 January raid that resulted in the death of three Marines.

The raids served multiple purposes. First, they were aimed at specific Iraqi artillery forces; second they were designed to confuse and bewilder the Iraqis by making the ultimate Marine breaching points unclear; and third they permitted Marine air to strike against the Iraqi artillery, considered Iraq's most dangerous conventional asset, which inevitably replied with counter-battery fire.

Each raid followed the same basic pattern. A Marine artillery battery would advance to the border and fire a carefully planned barrage. As soon as the shells cleared the barrels, they would "limber" the artillery pieces and drive away. Within minutes, the firing location would be

Marines of Task Force Shepherd plan their next operation. In addition to screening duties, the light armored infantry battalions also provided security for the Marine batteries conducting artillery raids on Iraqi forces in Kuwait.

empty desert. When Iraqi artillery attempted counter-battery fire, it would fall on the abandoned position, and waiting Marine air would pounce on the revealed Iraqi artillery and destroy it.

The composition of the raid forces followed a pattern as well. The ground element consisted of a battery of artillery with a small security force and a company of light armored vehicles from one of the light armored infantry battalions. The 3d Marine Aircraft Wing provided an aviation element: usually an OV-10 aircraft acting as an airborne forward air controller, a McDonnell Douglas F/A-18D Hornet and two Grumman A-6E Intruders to strike the enemy artillery sites, an F/A-18D and two McDonnell Douglas F/A-18 Hornets to suppress enemy air defenses, an F/A-18D as a forward air controller, and a Grumman EA-6B Prowler to provide electronic counter-measures support.[42]*

27-28 January

Despite the danger of Coalition air attacks, Saddam Hussein journeyed from Baghdad to the southern Iraqi city of al-Basrah on the morning of 27 January,

---
*The F/A-18D was a two seat version of the F/A-18. It was often used to perform coordination duties or to act as an airborne forward air controller.

where he met with two of his senior Iraqi officers in Kuwait, General Aeeid Khlel Zaky, commander of *IV Corps*, and General Salah Aboud Mahmoud commander of *III Corps*. Among others at the meeting was the Minister of Defense, the chief of staff, their deputies, other members of the general staff, and Colonel Aboud Haneed Mahoud, commander of Saddam's bodyguard.[43]

Al-Basrah's infrastructure was in ruins: "It was apparent on the road, which had big holes from the bombs and some destroyed military vehicles on the both side of the road," General Salah Aboud remembered. "In al-Basrah region all the damage was clear and we noticed it on the bridge, railroads, on the roads, on the facilities…. And the streets were very dark, compared to before the war, when they were glowing." At the military headquarters there was no power and small candles dimly lit the rooms. General Salah did not realize that he was to meet Saddam until he "saw the faces of the special guards."[44]

At the meeting, the Iraqi president presented the plan for the attack on al-Khafji and then gave his officers some words of inspiration. As General Hashem Sultan later recalled, Saddam began by discussing Iraqi military successes in the Iran-Iraq War. He said that success had come from Iraqi willpower, despite Iran's advantages in personnel and material. Then he discussed the Coalition air campaign against "our factories, cities, and roads." The air attacks had already lasted two weeks, he explained, because the Coalition did not have as much willpower as the Iranians and was afraid to fight a ground war against Iraq.[45]

He then told his officers that by inflicting casualties on the Coalition they would win the war, and save the lives of thousands of Iraqi citizens. Waiting was not to Iraq's advantage, they must do something now, implying that Iraq could not survive the continuous air bombardment. He concluded with an old Iraqi proverb: "In order to be ready to fight the fox, you must prepare to fight the lion."[46]

General Salah Aboud Mahmoud, given command of the al-Khafji mission, informed Saddam that he would present him with the city as a present on the morning of 30 January.[47] The meeting then broke up and the Iraqi president returned to Baghdad, surviving an attack by two U.S. Air Force General Dynamics F-16 Falcons. The Air Force did not realize they had hit Saddam's convoy until after the war.[48]

General Salah Aboud returned to Kuwait and met with his division and

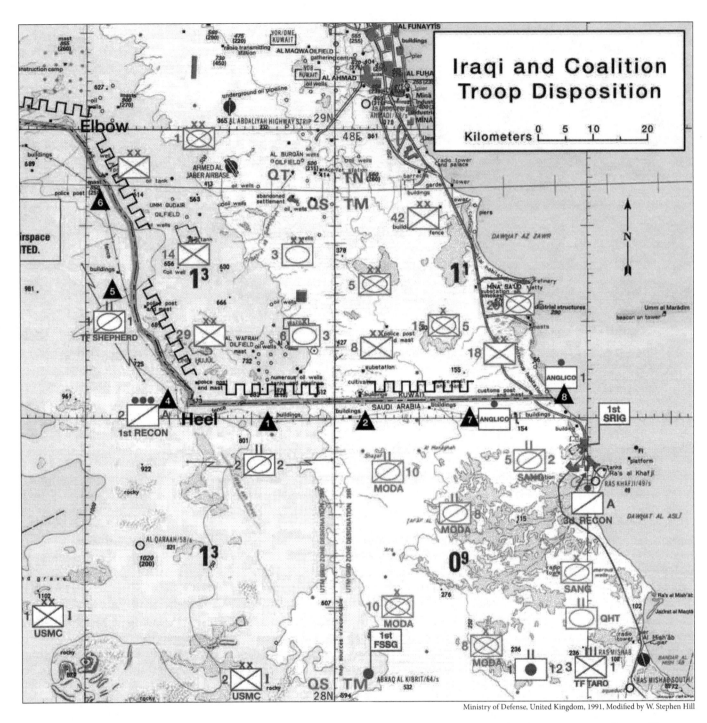

Ministry of Defense, United Kingdom, 1991, Modified by W. Stephen Hill

brigade commanders at the *5th Mechanized Division*'s headquarters, then at the oil facility of al-Maqoa. He instructed his commanders in tactics for countering Coalition airpower and ordered them to dig in quickly after reaching their objectives. He then passed on Saddam's inspirational words and told them of his promise to make Saddam a present of al-Khafji on the morning of 30 January. Finally, he approved *IV Corps'* request for artillery fire against the sector opposite the *7th Infantry* and *14th Infantry Divisions*. The Iraqi forces then began to move into position for the upcoming battle.[49]

Warnings

The Coalition did have some indications that the Iraqis were planning something. One of the E-8C Joint Surveillance and Target Acquisition Radar System aircraft reported large Iraqi vehicle movements on the night of 22 January, and again on 25 January. These were only preliminary Iraqi movements, but it also noted the Iraqi movement on the night of 28 January, which was the direct preparation for the upcoming offensive.[50]

All three of the observation posts manned by air-naval gunfire liaison Marines (Observation Posts 2, 7, and 8) reported unusually heavy Iraqi activity on the nights of 27 and 28 January. In addition, the Marines reported "sporadic Iraqi rocket and artillery fires were directed at the city of al-Khafji, the forward Saudi defensive belt, and the border observation posts, often with illumination rounds mixed in."[51] On the night of 27 January, Marines at Observation Post 7 called in a strike on Iraqi "mechanized reconnais-

12   The Battle of al-Khafji

sance forces" moving in front of their position, reporting two Iraqi armored personnel carriers destroyed.[52] Some Marine officers considered the Iraqi movements to be a response to the Marine artillery raids which had taken place on 21 and 26 January.[53]

On the night of 28 January the reported Iraqi mechanized movements coincided with another Marine artillery raid. The teams at the desalination plant north of al-Khafji, and at Observation Post 8, each called for airstrikes on Iraqi forces they observed, but the artillery raid just to the west had the priority for air support.[54] By 0315 on the 29th, the artillery raid had concluded and air support was again available to the observation post teams. At Observation Post 7, the air-naval gunfire supporting arms liaison team under Captain John C. Bley II called a flight of Fairchild-Republic A-10 Thunderbolt attack aircraft in on a column of Iraqi armored vehicles moving west across its front toward the al-Wafrah oil field. The Iraqi column suffered heavy damage; Bley's team reported nearly a dozen vehicles destroyed. The team observed Iraqi soldiers trying to recover vehicles at sunrise.[55] The team at Observation Post 2 also observed a large Iraqi force moving from east to west, which Coalition air power engaged. All three observation posts heard the movement of the Iraqi vehicles for the rest of the night.[56]

One Coalition officer who realized, at the time, that the Iraqis were preparing for an offensive was Lieutenant Colonel Richard M. Barry, commander of the forward headquarters of the 1st Surveillance, Reconnaissance, and Intelligence Group. He closely monitored Iraqi radio traffic during the airstrikes on 28 January and decided that "the Iraqis put probably 150 sappers out there to try and clear that road. [I] sensed they really wanted it opened. They were obviously using that road as some sort of interior line like at Gettysburg."[57] The information was passed on to higher headquarters. Lieutenant Colonel Barry was right; the air attacks against the *3d Armored Division* as it tried to pass through the Iraqi minefields of al-Wafrah paralyzed much of the division and General Salah Aboud spent much of 29 January trying to fix the scheduling problems these attacks caused.[58] When the division's attacks finally did fall on Observation Post 4 and Observation Post 1, they would be far weaker as a result.

Despite Lieutenant Colonel Barry's warning that "this is it …the Iraqis want Khafji," Central Command thought the possibility of an Iraqi ground attack remote as attention was focused on the air campaign and the expected ground offensive to liberate Kuwait.[59]

29 January

On the morning of 29 January, General Salah Aboud inspected the assembly areas of the *5th Mechanized Division*, and found fewer vehicles moving than he expected, many being broken down alongside the road. He also found that the division's deception operations were working well and he saw no sign that Coalition forces knew of its movements. He believed this was because "the order was given to take cover under the smoke clouds of the burning oil, and also the tanks, the armored personnel carriers, and the support weapons' vehicles were all deployed under the trees of al-Thal and were hard to see."[60]

Things were going worse with the *3d Armored Division*, especially with the division's *6th Armored Brigade* commanded by Colonel Ibdil Raziq Mahmoud. The brigade had been pounded by Coalition aircraft the night before and it had lost at least two tanks.

"On the morning of 29 January, the enemy started screaming and shouting after we completed deploying our forces in the desert area; although the enemy had their reconnaissance technologies they were not able to notice our forces," recalled Brigadier General Hussan Zedin commander of the *3d Armored Division*. He added: "[Coalition aircraft] started to attack our troops during the daylight, in their concealed locations. They tried to affect our morale and cause damage in order to make us too weak to execute the mission."[61]

The Marines of 2d Platoon, Company A, 1st Reconnaissance Battalion, would spend much of their time in the desert at Observation Post 4. Here they pose around an Iraqi T-55 tank captured on the morning of 30 January 1991.

Photo courtesy of MGySgt Gregory L. Gillispie

The Battle of al-Khafji

The air attacks led General Salah Aboud to conclude that the Coalition had discovered his brigade, and he expected it would face stiff resistance at its objectives. He told the *3d Armored Division* commander, Brigadier Commander Hussan Zedin, that the *6th Armored Brigade* could expect to face "tanks, anti-tank weapons, and armored cars." He ordered the brigade to employ "a reconnaissance assault a suitable distance ahead of the main convoy to get information about the strength of the resistance of the enemy."[62]

General Salah Aboud was wrong, however. Aside from Lieutenant Colonel Barry at 1st Surveillance, Reconnaissance, and Intelligence Group, the Coalition was not expecting an Iraqi attack, missing much of the Iraqi movement and interpreting the movement that it did observe as either training exercises or reactions to the Marine artillery raids. On the morning of 29 January, the Iraqi *III Corps* and *IV Corps* had moved to their assembly areas successfully. Coalition air power had already inflicted significant losses, but those losses had resulted from routine strikes in Kuwait and chance attacks against Iraqi forces caught moving in the open. The bulk of the Coalition's air effort remained focused elsewhere.

At al-Khafji, the various special operations and reconnaissance forces occupying the city were proceeding with what had become their normal day. For the air-naval gunfire liaison Marines, this meant routine relief of the forward positions. Captain Douglas R. Kleinsmith's supporting arms liaison team relieved Captain Bley and his team at Observation Post 7 in the early morning, and Bley's team returned to the group headquarters at the water desalination plant north of al-Khafji.

Less routine, but not surprising, was the capture of three Iraqi soldiers by Marines at Observation Post 8. All three were in clean uniforms, and appeared to be in good health, despite two weeks of Coalition airstrikes. First Lieutenant Kurtis E. Lang, commander of the air-naval gunfire team at the post, thought they were forward observers; the Iraqis carried maps that detailed Iraqi and some Coalition positions, including Observation Post 8. A U.S. Navy SEAL unit took charge of the prisoners and sent them to the rear. Approximately 30 minutes after the team captured the Iraqis, the enemy fired a single tank shell at the position, causing no damage.[63]

Along the coastal highway there were also indications of increased Iraqi activity. At Observation Post 7, Captain Kleinsmith reported Iraqi artillery six to eight kilometers in front of his position, while at Observation Post 8, Lieutenant Lang reported heavy vehicle noises.[64] At 2000, Captain Kleinsmith directed a successful A-6 attack on the two Iraqi artillery positions, eliminating at least one of the sites.[65]

Outposts

Observation Post 4 was a two-story Saudi police post known as Markaz al-Zabr. To the north, along the border ran a large berm approximately 15 feet high. The fort protected one of the few openings in the embankment.[66] On 29 January, Observation Post 4 was the only post this far west that was manned; it was held by 2d Platoon, Company A, 1st Reconnaissance Battalion, and a company of light armored vehicles.

The reconnaissance platoon had originally been Deep Reconnaissance Platoon, Company C, 3d Reconnaissance Battalion, based on Okinawa. Comprised of volunteers, it had shipped out to the Middle East in the initial rush to get Marines to Saudi Arabia in September 1990. With its parent battalion remaining on Okinawa, the platoon was absorbed into 1st Reconnaissance Battalion.[67]

Nearly two weeks before, the platoon, commanded by First Lieutenant Steven A. Ross, was assigned to Observation Post 4. Working as a platoon was a welcome change, since it had been previously assigned to various observation posts in smaller groups alongside other Marine reconnaissance and Army special forces teams. Supplies were running low, however, and the platoon was to be relieved on 30 January. Lieutenant Ross had dispersed his men along the berm, divided into three teams along a 500-meter front. Armed with M16 rifles, M249 squad automatic weapons, M60 machine guns, and M136 AT4 antitank weapons, the Marines were not equipped to stop a major Iraqi assault. Lieutenant Ross stationed the platoon's vehicles, four humvees and a 6x6 5-ton truck, behind a U-shaped berm approximately 500 meters to the rear of the observation post. In the event of a serious Iraqi attack, the plan was for the platoon to withdraw to the U-shaped berm, mount up, and move to the rear while calling in airstrikes on the Iraqis.[68]

Captain Roger L. Pollard's Company D, 3d Light Armored Infantry Battalion,

Marine Corps Art Collection

The Saudi border fort at Observation Post 4 was known as "OP Hamma" to some Marines. The painting by Capt Charles G. Grow depicts the oil fields at al-Wafrah on fire following a Coalition bombing raid on 24 January 1991.

Photo courtesy of MGySgt Gregory L. Gillispie

Maj Keith R. Kelly, Executive Officer, 1st Reconnaissance Battalion, and SSgt Gregory L. Gillispie, Platoon Sergeant, 2d Platoon, Company A, 1st Reconnaissance Battalion, pose at the southern end of their position on the berm at Observation Post 4. One of the platoon's bunkers can be seen to the right.

was attached to the 1st Light Armored Infantry Battalion, designated Task Force Shepherd. It had 19 General Dynamics LAV-25 light armored vehicles divided into two platoons and a company headquarters element.* Each LAV-25 was armed with an M242 Bushmaster 25mm cannon and carried a four-man infantry fire team. A section of seven General Dynamics LAV-AT light armored vehicles from 1st Light Armored Infantry Battalion's Headquarters Company was attached to Pollard's company. Each LAV-AT was equipped with an Emerson 901A1 TOW 2 [Tube launched, optically tracked, wire command link guided] antitank guided missile launcher, a thermal imaging system, and was manned by a crew of four. They were the company's primary antitank asset.[69]

At 1200, Company D was ordered to move to Observation Post 4 and act as a screen for the evening. Captain Pollard conducted a reconnaissance and established his company and its attached LAV-

Maj Jeffery A. Powers (left), operations officer of 1st Light Armored Infantry Battalion (Task Force Shepherd) and Capt Roger L. Pollard (right), commander of Company D, 3d Light Armored Infantry Battalion (Task Force Shepherd) examine the aftermath of the battle at Observation Post 4 on the morning of 30 January 1991.

Photo courtesy of Col Jeffrey A. Powers

AT section northwest of Observation Post 4 at around 1500. He created his fire plan, used a global positioning satellite device to precisely note his unit's location, and met with Lieutenant Ross. The liaison with Lieutenant Ross would prove to be incomplete, as Captain Pollard did not know that 2d Platoon had its own vehicles. This oversight would lead to misunderstandings during the engagement.[70]

Night, 29-30 January
At the Observation Posts

The first serious ground combat in the Battle of al-Khafji occurred at Observation Post 4. The *6th Armored Brigade* of the *3d Armored Division* was assigned to strike through the gap in the berm, drawing attention away from the movement of the *5th Mechanized Division* to the east. As General Salah Aboud later recalled: "The *6th Armored Brigade* was ordered to move forward from the heights above the al-Zabr [Observation Post 4] and they crossed the line at the eight o'clock at night. And at nine o'clock and thirty minutes they encountered enemy resistance at al-Zabr, in Saudi Arabia."[71]

---
*Standard light armored infantry company organization was three platoons and a headquarters element, but Company D had only four assigned officers. To compensate for the lack of officers, Captain Pollard organized the company into two platoons and trained the company to operate as two elements.

The Battle of al-Khafji   15

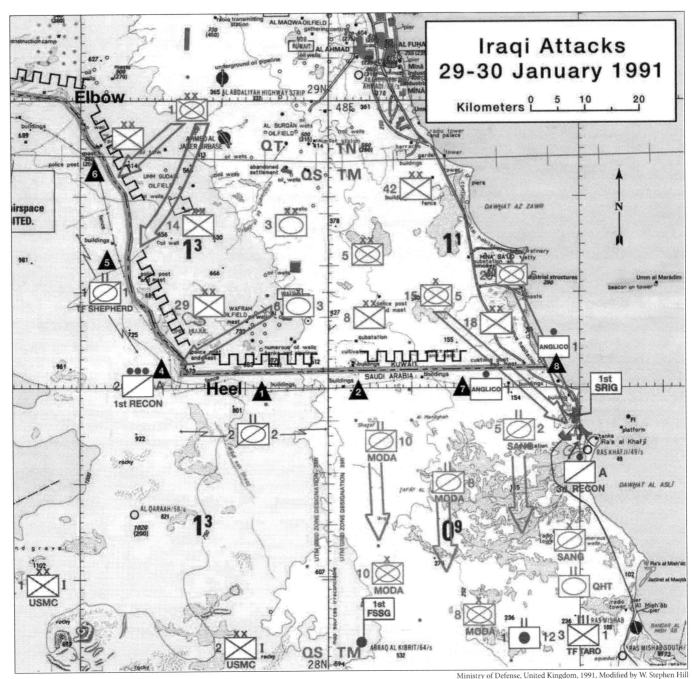

At 2000, Lieutenant Ross heard the clank of treads, then observed Iraqi armored vehicles advancing through his night-vision device; it was a sizeable force. He attempted to contact his outlying teams as well as Company D and the reconnaissance battalion headquarters by radio but got no response. Since contact earlier was no problem, there was a strong presumption that the reconnaissance platoon's radios were being jammed. Using runners, Lieutenant Ross alerted his platoon and continued trying to get through and inform higher headquarters and Company D of the oncoming Iraqi force.[72] Finally, at 2030, he made radio contact and informed Company D that a large mass of Iraqi vehicles, tanks, and armored personnel carriers, were advancing on Observation Post 4. Captain Pollard informed Task Force Shepherd and prepared his company to face the threat.[73]

At the observation post, there appeared to be some confusion within Ross' platoon. Rather than simply retreating to the U-shaped berm as planned, one of the teams opened fire on the oncoming Iraqi armor with machine guns and antitank weapons. At the ranges involved, there was very little chance that the Marines would do any damage to an Iraqi vehicles with their light antitank weapons. However, the fire startled the oncoming Iraqis, who slowed or stopped as they heard the "ping" of machine gun fire on their tank hulls. In response to the reconnaissance platoon's fire, the Iraqis began to fire back. Their fire was random and inaccurate, but the volume was impressive. At the same time, Iraqi communications jamming appeared to have stopped and Lieutenant Ross was able to re-establish radio contact with all three of his teams. He promptly ordered everyone to fall back to the U-shaped berm as previously arranged.[74]

To cover the reconnaissance platoon's withdrawal, Captain Pollard led his 2d

16 The Battle of al-Khafji

Photo courtesy of LtCol Charles H. Cureton

During the fight at Observation Post 4, LAV-AT "Green Two" was struck in the rear by an antitank missile fired by one of its fellows, causing the armored vehicle's magazine of 16 missiles to detonate with catastrophic results. Four Marines were lost with the vehicle: Cpl Ismael Cotto, PFC Scott A. Schroeder, LCpl David T. Snyder, and LCpl Daniel B. Walker.

Platoon's light armored vehicles forward, along with half of the LAV-ATs. The plan was for 2d Platoon to advance in line to aid the reconnaissance platoon, while the LAV-ATs conducted a "bounding overwatch." The LAV-AT had to stop when they fired. In order to provide cover for the advancing LAV-ATs and LAV-25s, half of the LAV-ATs would stop, ready to fire, while the others advanced a short way. The second group would then stop and cover the first group as they advanced, and so on. During the advance, after receiving permission, one of the LAV-ATs fired its antitank missile on what it believed to be an Iraqi tank. Instead, the missile hit "Green Two," one of its fellows, a few hundred yards to its front.[75]

The missile penetrated the rear hatch of the armored vehicle and detonated the 16 missiles stored in the rear compartment, completely destroying it in a huge fireball and killing its crew.[76] "It came through the bottom, right, troop hatch on this one," Lieutenant David Kendall of Company D later said. It "hit all the other missiles, I guess, and it was all a spontaneous detonation. There were no secondary explosions. Nothing. This whole thing just went up."[77]

There was confusion at this point, with some Company D Marines believing the vehicle had been destroyed by Iraqi tank fire and others not certain the vehicle had actually been destroyed. The explosion obliterated it so completely that there was not enough wreckage left to register on night vision devices. The crew did not respond to radio calls, but it was common for a radio to cease working. The fate of the LAV-AT would not be confirmed until the next morning.[78]

Captain Pollard and his 2d Platoon continued forward, leaving the LAV-ATs behind. He was finally informed that Ross' platoon had sufficient vehicles to withdraw. Pollard's platoon halted and began firing on the Iraqi vehicles with their 25mm guns. The reconnaissance platoon had observed the incident and

Two LAV-ATs from 1st Light Armored Infantry Battalion drive across the Saudi desert. The LAV-AT provided the heavy fire power of the battalion with its antitank missiles.

History Division Photo

An Air Force A-10A Thunderbolt patrols over the desert during the Gulf War. The aircraft carried AGM 65 Maverick air-to-ground missiles and was one of the primary providers of close air support during the Battle of al-Khafji.

Lieutenant Ross was convinced that Company D would soon fire on his troops by mistake as well. He ordered the platoon to mount its vehicles and withdraw from the battlefield.

After Ross' platoon had completed its withdrawal, Company D's 1st Platoon shifted south of the 2nd Platoon in order to support 2d Platoon's fire against the Iraqi forces advancing on the now-abandoned observation post. Pollard's company then backed away from the border but continued to engage the Iraqi armor with missile and 25mm cannon fire. Although the fire had little hope of damaging the Iraqi vehicles at the ranges involved, it served to disorient the Iraqi tanks, which stopped and buttoned up as the rounds ricocheted off their armor. The fire was also useful for marking Iraqi vehicles for incoming aircraft. The company's executive officer, First Lieutenant Scott P. Williams, and Corporal Russell T. Zawalick, acted as forward air controllers for a series of air strikes against the Iraqi forces, using this method of marking the enemy.[79]

The battle at the observation post was now under control as Coalition air support arrived in large numbers. "At that point, everything was going pretty well." Lieutenant Kendall later noted, "We started getting the air in. It was hitting the tanks down there, and we were just marking for the air by firing our main guns at the tanks and they were following the tracer rounds to them and hitting them with the air."[80] Hearing reports of some Iraqi tanks attempting to cross the berm further south, Captain Pollard withdrew the company approximately 5,000 meters from the observation post.

A section of Air Force A-10 Thunderbolts then arrived over the battlefield. Corporal Zawalick was controlling air support with live ammunition for the first time, but under Lieutenant Williams' guidance, he directed the incoming aircraft to their targets. But the A-10s were finding it difficult to identify the Iraqis. After two failed attempts, a Thunderbolt dropped a flare, which landed next to "Red Two," one of the company's LAV-25s. Corporal Zawalick informed the A-10 the flare had marked a friendly position, and directed him toward the enemy from the flare. Meanwhile, a rifleman jumped from "Red Two" to bury the flare, but as he did so the A-10 fired an AGM 65 Maverick air-to-ground missile which struck the LAV-25, destroying it and killing all of the crew that remained inside save the driver, who was ejected from the vehicle.[81] The investigation con-

An American flag flies from the burnt hulk of "Red Two," which was destroyed by a malfunctioning air-to-surface antitank missile during the fight at Observation Post 4. Seven Marines were lost with the vehicle: LCpl Frank C. Allen, Cpl Stephen E. Bentzlin, LCpl Thomas A. Jenkins, LCpl Michael E. Linderman, Jr., LCpl James H. Lumpkins, Sgt Garett A. Mongrella, and LCpl Dion J. Stephenson.

Photo courtesy of Sgt Mark S. McDonnell

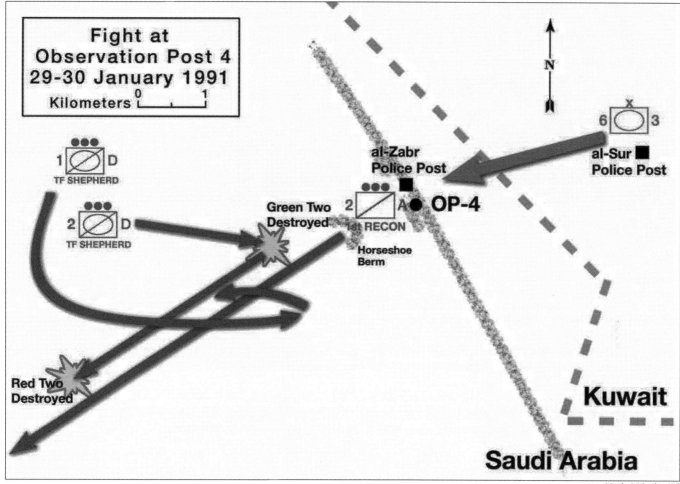

Map by W. Stephen Hill

ducted by I Marine Expeditionary Force after the battle determined that the most likely cause of the incident was a malfunction by the Maverick missile.[82]

Again there was confusion as Pollard tried to determine if "Red Two" had been destroyed by friendly or enemy fire. "That's the first time, the first time I got scared," he later remembered. "I didn't know what had happened. I didn't know where the bad guys were."[83] There was some worry that the Iraqis had penetrated the berm and succeeded in out-flanking the company. As a result, Pollard reorganized the company into a screen line and pulled it back slowly.[84]

"The Marines, of that company, as the whole battalion, were calm," said the commander of Task Force Shepherd, Lieutenant Colonel Clifford O. Myers III. "All of my conversations with Captain Pollard… were extremely calm and in total control. Even after the Maverick hit 'em."[85]

Despite the calm demeanor that Lieutenant Colonel Myers observed, Pollard's company had lost one vehicle to fire from its own air support and another was missing. With massive amounts of air support moving to the border, and other companies ready and able to move into contact, Lieutenant Colonel Myers ordered Company D to withdraw to the west and link up with Task Force Shepherd's Company A, commanded by Captain Michael A. Shupp. Company D accomplished the maneuver shortly after midnight on the 30th. The remaining six LAV-ATs were transferred to Company A, and Company D was reorganized and resupplied behind Shupp's company, which moved forward to screen Observation Post 4.[86]

The Iraqi perspective on the battle's outcome at the observation post differed considerably from the American view. "Now this small [enemy] force consisted of armored vehicles equipped with a large number of the antitank weapons and the brigade informed us they had destroyed a number of tanks, stopping the brigade convoy," General Salah Aboud remembered. "So, I ordered those fighting the enemy, to stop the enemy forces and let the brigade pass this resistance to the east, and to move towards the brigade target without stopping. [The] 6th Armored Brigade moved deep into Saudi Arabia and the small resisting force was rolled over and the brigade caused a large amount of damage."[87] There is no evidence that the flanking movement General Salah described penetrated more than a few hundred meters into Saudi Arabia, and the *3d Armored Division's* commander did not mention it. "Although, our troops continued by moving towards the targets, we faced a very strong ground resistance at al-Zabr supported by the Air Force and helicopters from the enemy." As Brigadier General Hussan Zedin reported: "At 8 o 'clock on 29 January, we executed our duty and we stayed in the area until the forces of Mohammad Al Qasim completed their duty and mission to occupy al-Khafji."[88] *

Whether or not it had entered into Saudi Arabia, the *6th Armored Brigade* had accomplished its primary mission.

---

* "Mohammad Al Qasim" was the honorific name for the *5th Mechanized Division*.

Photo courtesy of MGySgt Gregory L. Gillispie

The remains of two of the 6th Armored Brigade's T-62 tanks, destroyed on the night of 29 January 1991, lie abandoned on the sand in front of Observation Post 4. The Iraqis suffered severe materiel and equipment losses during the four-day Battle of al-Khafji.

"All the airplanes of the enemy were over the brigade convoy and attacking the area," as General Salah explained. "The brigade had succeeded in capturing completely the attention of the enemy. And the enemy didn't observe any movement of our troops to occupy al-Khafji so at midnight, I instructed the 3d Armored Division to order the 6th Armored Brigade to go back towards Al Wahfra and their original positions."[89]

Supported by air, the Marines of a light armored vehicle company and a reconnaissance platoon had stopped the attack of an Iraqi armored brigade in its tracks. The two units suffered 11 casualties, none of which was from enemy fire. The Marines at Observation Post 4 had not experienced combat before the attack on 29 January.

While the fight at Observation Post 4 was taking place, a brigade of the *5th Mechanized Division* attempted to cross into Saudi Arabia through the berm near Observation Post 1, then screened by Company A, 2d Light Armored Infantry Battalion, commanded by Captain Dennis M. Greene. At 2115, it observed "60-100 BMPs [armored personnel carriers]…moving south with arty."* The company called in air, reporting that AV-8s and A-10s engaged the Iraqi forces.[90] The company then observed a 29-vehicle column of Iraqi armor arriving at the berm. At 2320, Corporal Edmund W. Willis III knocked out one of the Iraqi T-62 tanks with an antitank missile.[91]

Greene's company continued to act as forward air controllers for strikes on the Iraqi forces moving across the berm throughout the evening. It received a significant amount of air power: five A-6s, two F-16s, two A-10s, and eight AV-8s, and reported 11 destroyed vehicles. Corporal Willis fired another missile at 0157, hitting the same T-62 as the Iraqis attempted to move it to the rear.[92] At around the same time, the Iraqis halted their attack and retreated back into Kuwait.[93]

Further north, Company C, 1st Light Armored Infantry Battalion established a screen between Observation Post 6 and Observation Post 5. Commanded by Captain Thomas R. Protzeller, it had a section of LAV-ATs attached, similar to Pollard's company at Observation Post 4. But unlike Company D, it had a section of General Dynamics LAV-Ms (a light armored vehicle variant armed with an M252 81mm mortar) attached. Originally, Protzeller's company screen line centered on Observation Post 5, but early on the evening of 29 January, the company had fired its mortars at suspected Iraqi forward observers. As a result, Major Jeffrey A. Powers, Task Force Shepherd's operations officer, ordered the company to withdraw from the berm in order to forestall any retaliatory Iraqi artillery fire.[94]

Protzeller's company observed the

A Marine LAV-AT is positioned behind the sand berm that separated Saudi Arabia from Kuwait. Built to control the wanderings of nomadic Bedouin tribesmen, the berm offered a convenient demarcation of the border between Saudi Arabia and Kuwait. Observation Post 5 can be seen in the background.

Photo courtesy of Cpl Kenneth J. Lieuwen

---

* Most sources confuse Observation Post 1 and Observation Post 2, but according to both the 2d Light Armored Infantry Battalion's command chronology, and the 1st ANGLICO's after action report, Observation Post 1 was in 2d Light Armored Infantry Battalion's area of operations and Observation Post 2 was in the Joint Forces Command-East area of operations. Most likely, this confusion resulted from the use of two conflicting methods of numbering the border observation posts. Originally, U.S. Army Special Forces teams numbered the observation posts as they occupied them, in chronological sequence rather than geographic sequence. The Marines later attempted to regularize the observation post designations, but the new system did not stick and only served to confuse the issue.

Photo courtesy of Cpl Kenneth J. Lieuwen
Iraqi prisoners of war huddle near a fire to keep warm, while Marines of Task Force Shepherd examine the prisoner's weapons, an AK-74, RPK-74, two pistols, and two grenades. Although some prisoners were captured by Marine and Saudi forces during the Battle of al-Khafji, they did not surrender in the vast numbers taken during the later advance into Kuwait.

fighting taking place to the south around Observation Post 4, but did not take part in the fight until around 2230 when it was ordered to occupy Observation Post 5 as a blocking force. Shortly thereafter, the company was informed that approximately 70 enemy vehicles were moving toward Observation Post 6, and it was ordered to block that position. Traveling along the berm, Protzeller's company advanced north cautiously; each platoon took turns covering the other. As it advanced the company fired antitank missiles at a group of Iraqi vehicles it spotted on the Saudi side of the berm. Once the company reached Observation Post 6, around 0100, it settled in and called airstrikes on the Iraqi infantry, who had occupied the post and on their vehicles that had retreated back to the Kuwaiti side of the berm. In the morning, many of the demoralized Iraqi soldiers surrendered with little fuss, others having apparently withdrawn.[95]

The 2d Light Armored Infantry Battalion's fight at Observation Post 1, and Company C, 1st Light Armored Infantry Battalion's fight at Observation Post 6 both ended early on the morning on 30 January, but the enemy made one last gasp at Observation Post 4 just after the sun rose at 0720. There Task Force Shepherd's Company A, under Captain Shupp, called in airstrikes from Air Force A-10s and Marine Corps F/A-18s. The air attack smashed this final Iraqi advance at the outpost.[96]

At dawn, Company A established a screen on the berm while Company D recovered its dead and secured Iraqi prisoners. The morning light revealed fully the destruction caused in the previous evenings fight. Pollard's company and its attached LAV-AT section had lost 11 Marines and two vehicles in the five hour battle at Observation Post 4, but destroyed approximately 22 Iraqi tanks and armored personnel carriers and killed scores of Iraqi soldiers. When the recovery effort was complete, Company A withdrew and Company D reestablished its position at Observation Post 4, which it was to hold for another 10 days.[97]

Assault on al-Khafji

At Observation Post 2, Captain David W. Landersman and his air-naval gunfire team heard a large number of vehicle noises approaching their position. Keenly aware of the fight at Observation Post 4 to their west, they requested air support but abandoned the outpost before the air support could be diverted from the fight at the western observation post.[98] Meanwhile, Iraqi artillery began firing on Captain Kleinsmith and his team at Observation Post 7, as well as south along the coast road. The two teams reported that the artillery fire was a combination of illumination and high explosive rounds.[99]

As Captain Kleinsmith's team was being shelled by the Iraqis, a mechanized Iraqi force attacked Observation Post 8 and Lieutenant Lang's team with "intense direct machine gun, recoilless rifle, and tank main gun fire."[100] Three different groups were stationed at Observation Post 8: Lang's fire control team team; a U.S. Navy SEAL detachment; and a team from 3d Force Reconnaissance Company. "After numerous illumination rounds, pop-up flares, and mortar rounds Fire Control Team 9 [FCT], south of OP-8, was overrun by APCs [armored person-

The Battle of al-Khafji

21

nel carriers] with the SEALs from OP-8 retreating just in front of the enemy APCs."[101] Despite the heavy fire, all three teams managed to evade the Iraqi assault and fell back without suffering casualties. The SEAL and reconnaissance teams pulled back to al-Mishab, and Lieutenant Lang's team joined 1st Surveillance, Reconnaissance, and Intelligence Group at the desalination plant.[102]

Three Saudi battalions had formed a screen along the Kuwaiti border in Joint Forces Command-East's area of operations. Their orders, according to General Khaled, were clear: "to observe the movement of Iraqi troops and report the approach of hostile columns. They were not to engage the enemy or risk being taken prisoner. I did not want to give Saddam a propaganda victory. If the Iraqis crossed the border, they were to rejoin our main force further south."[103]

The 5th Mechanized Battalion of the 2d Saudi Arabian National Guard Brigade, commanded by Lieutenant Colonel Naif, had responsibility for the coast road and the surrounding area. The road itself was not covered; the vehicle assigned to it was repositioned closer to the rest of the unit, and the battalion was not in communication with the various American forces stationed in al-Khafji and the border observation posts. As the battalion advanced down the coast road, it came under enemy artillery fire, and pulled back before the Iraqi advance without offering any resistance. Two battalions from the 8th and 10th Saudi Arabian National Guard Brigades, screening further inland, executed similar movements.[104] Unopposed by ground forces, the Iraqi *15th Mechanized Brigade* drove south into al-Khafji, although it was struck by an Air Force Lockheed AC-130 Spectre gunship and Marine AH-1W Super Cobras.[105]

"As the APCs overran the forward position tank main gun and mortar rounds began impacting in the area of the desalinization plant that SALT 5 [Supporting Arms Liaison Team 5] and SRIG [Surveillance, Reconnaissance, and Intelligence Group] forward occupied," Captain James R. Braden of 1st ANGLICO explained. "SRIG [Surveillance, Reconnaissance, and Intelligence Group] forward ordered all teams in the city to pull out and head for the 'safehouse' in al-Khafji. A hasty meeting was held just south of the desalinization plant between FCT 9 [Fire Control Team 9] and SALT 5 [Supporting Arms Liaison Team 5] to conduct a head count and confirm the rendezvous at the safehouse in the southern part of the city of Khafji."[106]

Lieutenant Colonel Barry's group and Lieutenant Lang's team withdrew from the desalination plant to the southern outskirts of al-Khafji and established an observation post in a water tower, but the advancing *15th Mechanized Brigade* forced the units to withdraw again. Barry's group headed south to al-Mishab, while Lieutenant Lang's team rejoined other 1st ANGLICO teams with the Qatari brigade.[107]

Stationed on the east side of al-Khafji, near the beach, was a unit of Saudi Marines. Designed to emulate U.S. Marines, this newly formed Saudi force lacked equipment and their American Marine advisors who had not yet joined them. As Captain Molofsky later explained, they were "camped out—basically functioning at very low ebb."[108] Joint Forces Command-East ordered the unit to withdraw just after midnight to al-Mishab and they took no further part in the battle.[109]

At this point in the battle, some bitterness arose on the part of the Saudis concerning the amount of air support being allocated to Joint Forces Command-East forces. In the face of the Iraqi advance, Major General Sultan "repeatedly called on the U.S. Marine Corps for air strikes to stop them." As General Khaled later recounted: "He was in close touch with the Marines because they shared a sector. They had trained together and an American liaison officer was attached to his headquarters. But in spite of his pleas, no air strikes had taken place. Coalition aircraft had not moved."[110] The resentment can be attributed in part to poor communications. Shortly after midnight, Major General Sultan had called for airstrikes against the *15th Mechanized Brigade* as it

During exercises prior to the beginning of the war, Marines rush to load antitank missiles onto an AH-1W Cobra of HMLA 369. The Cobras provided extensive close air support during the Battle of al-Khafji, both at the observation post battles and in the town proper.
History Division Photo

drove south to al-Khafji. He claimed "that there had been no air attack," when in fact an attack had taken place against the Iraqi column.[111] But primarily the Saudi impatience arose from differing priorities. The Americans viewed the Iraqi occupation of al-Khafji as a minor inconvenience that would soon be rectified, but for the Saudi kingdom it was an assault on their own sacred soil.

Saudi impatience could explain the perception of lack of air support, as well as inexperience in modern air-ground cooperation that the battle required. However, the Marines working alongside Joint Forces Command-East also supported the Saudi belief. As Captain Braden later wrote: "Little air support was available to the [Joint Forces Command-East] forces as the priority of effort was with the Marines to the west in repulsing the attack of the Iraqi *1st Mechanized Division* and elements of the *3d Armored Division*. The Marine fight had preceded the JFCE fight by a couple of hours and would remain the focus of effort throughout the night."[112]

The fight at Observation Post 4 attracted the attention of Coalition aircraft right away. A later Air Force study found: "Marine and Air Force CAS [Close Air Support] began to arrive in front of OP-4 by 2130 local time. By 2300, three AC-130 gunships, two F-15Es, two … F-16Cs, and four A-10s had joined the battle at OP-4."[113] Despite the rapid response to the fighting at Observation Post 4, all sources agree that the tactical air control center did not respond promptly to the initial Iraqi attacks. By most accounts, it was not until Brigadier General Buster C. Glosson, the director of campaign plans, entered the center on a routine check of current operations that someone thought to wake up Lieutenant General Charles A. Horner, the Joint Force Air Component Commander. Prior to that time, although the 3d Marine Aircraft Wing had responded to Marine calls for air support with alacrity, the tactical air control center remained focused on the evening's strikes into Iraq. Once awakened, General Horner realized that this was a major Iraqi offensive, and a wonderful opportunity to strike at Iraqi forces while they were on the move and vulnerable. He refocused the Coalition air effort into Kuwait accordingly.[114]

Much of the Marine air support for al-Khafji fell on the Cobras of Marine Light Attack Helicopter Squadron 369, commanded by Lieutenant Colonel Michael M. Kurth, and Marine Light Attack Helicopter Squadron 367, commanded by Lieutenant Colonel Terry J. Frerker.[115] Because the arrangement with Joint Forces Air Component Command left Marine helicopters totally in support of the Marine air-ground task force, the Cobras were able to respond rapidly to the Iraqi offensive. Eight AH-1W Cobras responded to initial calls from the air-naval gunfire liaison Marines, ensuring that the Iraqi advance into al-Khafji was not unopposed. Not long after 0100 on the 30th, a flight of four Cobras from Kurth's squadron, led by Major Michael L. Steele, engaged in a gun duel with six Iraqi armored personnel carriers on the coast road, reportedly pitting the helicopters' 20mm Gatling guns and 2.75mm rockets against the armored personnel carriers' 73mm main guns.[116]

Two AH-1Ws from Frerker's squadron, led by Major Gary D. Shaw, had an even more hair-raising experience. Launching from al-Mishab to provide air support at Observation Post 4, they found themselves circling and waiting for a forward air controller to provide them with targets. Eager to support the Marines on the ground, they over stayed their fuel limits and attempted to reach the logistics base at Kibrit, only to find themselves flying over an Iraqi armored column which fired on them. They then attempted to divert back to al-Mishab, but their navigation equipment malfunctioned and they landed instead at the al-Khafji oil refinery. This was a stroke of luck. They refueled their aircraft from the refinery's supplies as the Iraqis marched into the city. The unidentified fuel worked well and they were able to return to base.[117]

Another flight of Cobras, led by Captain Randal W. Hammond, destroyed four T-62 tanks. When nine Iraqi soldiers waved white flags and indicated they wished to surrender, they used their helicopters to "round 'em up like cattle" until Marines on the ground could secure the prisoners. Iraqi artillery fire forced the section to withdraw, but not before one Cobra destroyed a final T-62 with a wire-guided missile. The explosion caused "its turret to flip upside down and land on the open hole like a tiddlywinks," Captain Hammond later recalled.[118]

A little after noon on the 29th, the Iraqis also dispatched 15 fast patrol boats from Ras al-Qulayah, as a U.S. Marine raiding force was taking Maradim Island. Apparently intending to land commandos at al-Khafji in support of *5th Mechanized Division*, the Iraqi boats were intercepted by Royal Air Force SEPECAT GR-1A Jaguar aircraft and Royal Navy Westland HMA.8 Lynx helicopters from HMS *Brazen, Cardiff,* and *Gloucester.* Other Coalition aircraft then continued the attack, destroying or severely damaging all of the Iraqi boats and landing forces.[119]

At Observation Post 7, Captain Kleinsmith continued to call for fire while forming a defensive perimeter with the U.S. Army Special Forces and Marine 3d Force Reconnaissance teams. An OV-10 Bronco arrived over the battlefield and worked with Captain Kleinsmith as the airborne forward air controller. He found it difficult to control airstrikes because the location of friendly forces was unclear. Looking north of the border, Captain Kleinsmith directed Intruder and Harrier sections in a strike against Iraqi artillery positions, while a flight of Cobras circled above. He thought the Cobras would prevent his team from being overrun as Observation Post 8 had been, and he was "trusting that their sheer intimidation would keep the enemy away from his position." But as the Cobras circled overhead, the soldiers and Marines listened as Iraqi vehicles moved in the darkness around their position.[120]

Captain Kleinsmith had been kept informed as the other air-naval gunfire teams withdrew through al-Khafji. When the Cobras circling above his position were forced to return to base due to low fuel, Captain Kleinsmith and the leaders of the other two teams at Observation Post 7 decided there was little reason to remain in place. The Special Forces team had two escape and evasion routes planned: one east to the coastal highway and then south to al-Khafji; the other traveling west to Observation Post 2 and then south across the desert. Both routes appeared to be cut off by Iraqi forces, so Captain Kleinsmith led the teams' humvees south, directly into the *sabkhas*. He hoped the heavier Iraqi armor would

Photo courtesy of LtCol Douglas R. Kleinsmith

Capt Douglas R. Kleinsmith poses with his air-ground liaison team. Capt Kleinsmith is on the left, and to the right are Cpl John D. Calhoun, Cpl Steve F. Foss, and Cpl Edward E. Simons, Jr. On the night of 29-30 January 1991 Kleinsmith's team was cut off from Coalition forces by the Iraqi advance. They evaded the enemy by maneuvering through the sabkhas *and returned to Coalition lines.*

not follow them into the salt marsh.[121]

The teams departed at 0230 as Iraqi artillery fire briefly pursued them. They suffered no casualties. Kleinsmith's group remained in radio contact with the OV-10, which was now free to call in airstrikes around the observation post. As it drove south it discovered "the remnants of the SANG [Saudi Arabian National Guard] screening force camps, complete with boiling tea on the fires just outside their tents."[122] At approximately 0330, Kleinsmith ordered a halt, worried that the teams might come under friendly fire if they attempted to join up with a Saudi unit in the darkness. They remained deep in the salt marshes until daybreak.[123]

The Iraqi View

At 1800 on 29 January, General Salah Aboud shifted from his main headquarters to his mobile headquarters so he could better control the upcoming battle. Despite Coalition air attacks, as night fell on the 29th the Iraqi offensive was progressing according to plan. At 2000, the various brigades of the *5th Mechanized*, *1st Mechanized*, and *3d Armored Divisions* crossed their lines of departure and began the attack. As General Salah Aboud later observed: "The troops faced some difficulties executing these missions. The territory of one mission faced the road, which was hard for all the mechanized equipments to use, and for that reason, this mechanized brigade didn't have another choice, except to occupy their targets by walking. Still, all the troops reached the targets on time. And this actually deceived the enemy."[124]

In particular, the *15th Mechanized* and *26th Mechanized Brigades* of the *5th Mechanized Division* passed through Ragawa at 2000. At this point, the Iraqi artillery began firing flares that they could use to navigate through the desert. While moving into position they observed the withdrawal of Coalition forces from the border observation posts.[125] Although the Iraqi mechanized forces had difficulties in the *sabkhas*, they reached their objectives on time. A convoy from the *22d Mechanized Brigade* met no resistance at Saudi border stations, and its arrival along the beach completed the encirclement of al-Khafji. The *26th Mechanized Brigade*, encountering no resistance, returned to its positions in Kuwait after its role of defending the Western flank of the *15th Mechanized Brigade* was complete.[126]

General Salah Aboud kept his promise, delivering the city of al-Khafji at 0200 on the 30th as a present to Saddam Hussein. The supporting attacks had all run into heavy resistance and been stopped with high loss of life, but al-Khafji was in Iraqi hands. Now the Iraqis had to decide how long they needed to hold the city in order to accomplish their objective of provoking a major ground war.

The Iraqi Army Chief of Staff then contacted General Salah Aboud and asked for his predictions and recommendations. The general replied that "when the enemy discovers the size of my force, he will focus his air effort on it," but that "the time we have until morning will not be enough to pull back from al-Khafji." General Salah recommended that his troops pull back the next night, the evening of the 30-31 January, "after this great victory we achieved without any damage." He noted "the first night was passed without any specific operations from the enemy side."[127]

Although the Iraqis occupied al-Khafji, they were not alone. The 3d

24   The Battle of al-Khafji

Marines had a pair of reconnaissance teams in the city on 29 January; they had not left with the air-naval gunfire and special operations forces. They were in contact with their platoon commander, Captain Daniel K. Baczkowski, at 3d Marines' headquarters, who had informed the 3d Marines commander, Colonel John Admire, of the teams' locations. Colonel Admire ordered the teams to remain in place.[128]

Corporal Lawrence M. Lentz commanded a seven-man team comprising Corporals Scott A. Uskoski, Scott A. Wagner, Lance Corporals Marcus C. Slavenas, Alan L. Cooper, Jr., Jude A. Woodarek, and Hospital Mate Carlos Dayrit. Corporal Charles H. Ingraham III commanded a six-man team consisting of Corporal Jeffery D. Brown, Lance Corporals Harold S. Boling, David S. McNamee, Patrick A. Sterling, and Hospital Mate 1st Class Kevin Callahan. The teams were part of 3d Platoon, Company A, 3d Reconnaissance Battalion. Company A had been attached to 1st Reconnaissance Battalion for Operations Desert Shield and Storm.[129]

The intent of the 3d Marines' staff was that these teams, hidden within the town, would provide a valuable view of the city during a counterattack. However, in practice they were a liability, as Captain Molofsky later explained. Their presence affected the "ability to conduct the counter-attack, because we're not even sure where they're at," he said. "They did not even have restricted fire areas around them. Well, maybe they did, maybe they didn't. But that wasn't translated to us, so that when we want to do this counter attack and want to prep it with artillery; we don't know where the Recon teams are."[130]

The teams were not aware of these issues. They carefully prepared their observation posts, set out claymore mines in case the Iraqis discovered their positions, and attempted to call artillery fire and airstrikes on the Iraqi forces they observed. They were not always successful; artillery support was sometimes refused because the teams did not know where Saudi or air-naval gunfire units were, and air support was still being sent primarily to the fight at Observation Post 4.[131]

30 January

By the morning of the 30th, the fierce battles of the night before had ended. It became clear that the Iraqis had halted, and while the fighting had been intense for those at the front, for the I Marine Expeditionary Force staff the Iraqi offensive left a feeling of bemusement. At the morning briefing on the 30th, General Boomer observed: "Other than our losses, I am not unhappy with last night. It proceeded as it should.... My only concern is that we get something out to kill [the Iraqi force] before it gets back up into Kuwait."[132] "I believe that my feeling," he said later, "was that if they're trying that now, they're going to play right into our hands.... Then as it became clear that they were trying to do something of significance we began to react. I think by that point the MEF staff was at the point where it could handle this kind of thing without it being some huge crisis."[133]

General Khaled had a less sanguine view of the invasion. The Saudis understood how easily Saddam could turn even a battlefield disaster into a propaganda victory. They simply could not accept the loss of Saudi territory, even for a short while. When he received the news of the attack he "felt a great deal of anxiety."[134] King Fahd ibn Abdul Aziz of Saudi Arabia was often in contact. "King Fahd wanted quick results, and rightly so. He wanted the enemy force expelled at once. He wished to deny Saddam the chance of showing the world that he could invade Saudi Arabia and get away with it. He telephoned me a number of times, calling for action."[135] Faced with such pressure General Khaled did not consider al-Khafji a minor skirmish.

As dawn broke in the *sabkha* west of al-Khafji, Captain Kleinsmith's small caravan spotted unidentified tanks in the distance. His men mounted up and proceeded

Cpl Charles H. Ingraham's reconnaissance team used this building in al-Khafji throughout the battle as their observation post. Although the team was not discovered by the Iraqis, the building was hit by fire from Iraqis and Saudis during the night engagements, as well as shrapnel from American air and artillery strikes.

Photo courtesy of Cpl Charles H. Ingraham III

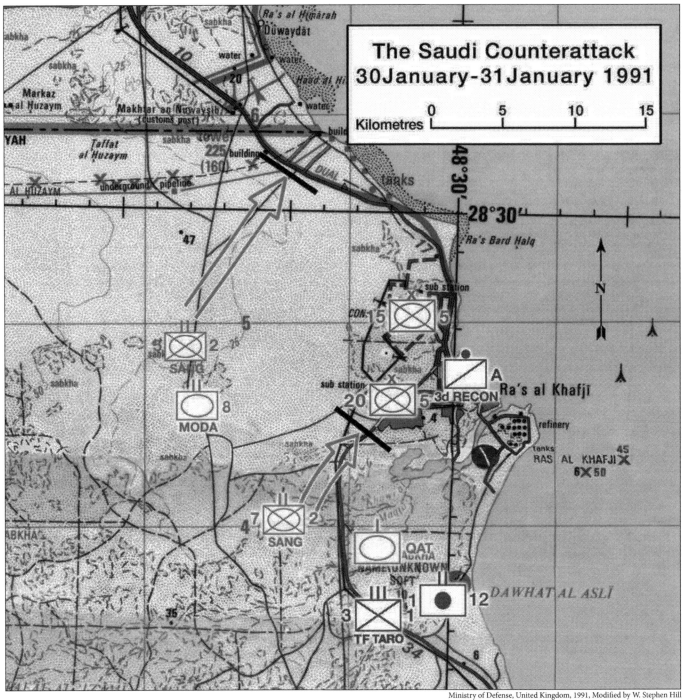

Ministry of Defense, United Kingdom, 1991, Modified by W. Stephen Hill

south to Saudi Arabian lines. At this point, the Special Forces and 3d Force Reconnaissance teams departed for al-Mishab, while Captain Kleinsmith and his Marines moved to the 2d Saudi Arabian National Guard Brigade headquarters, joining the main body of 1st ANGLICO.[136]

Meanwhile, other 1st ANGLICO teams were spread among the Saudi and Qatari forces that were preparing to retake the city and push the Iraqis back into Kuwait. Captain Mark S. Gentil's Supporting Arms Liaison Team 5, First Lieutenant Bruce D. McIlvried's Fire Control Team 13, and First Lieutenant Kurtis E. Lang's Fire Control Team 9 were assigned to the Qatari Brigade, commanded by Lieutenant Colonel Ali Saeed. Each of the fire control teams joined with one of the brigade's battalions, while the supporting arms liaison team acted as the fire support coordinator. Each battalion had a company of AMX-30 tanks attached as well.[137]

Captain James R. Braden's Supporting Liaison Team 6 was attached to Colonel Turki al-Firmi's 2d Saudi Arabian National Guard Brigade. Captain Braden's team acted as a central clearing house for all supporting fire and allowed Colonel Turki to use the Marine communications net to keep track of his battalions. Fire Control Team 12, commanded by Captain John C. Bley II, was assigned to the 8th Battalion, 2d Saudi National Guard Brigade, along with Captain Mark V. Dillard's team from Supporting Arms Liaison Team 2. Dillard's team originally was assigned to a Moroccan unit south of al-Mishab but was called forward to assist in the battle.[138]

Responsible for the defense of al-Khafji and the coastal region, Saudi

26   The Battle of al-Khafji

Major General Sultan 'Adi al-Matiri's initial plan of action was to cut off the Iraqi forces in al-Khafji and convince them to surrender. His intention was to avoid a potentially costly battle within the city.[139] To this end he dispatched the 5th Battalion, 2d Saudi Arabian National Guard Brigade, north of al-Khafji as a blocking force, supported by a company from the 8th Ministry of Defense and Aviation Brigade, equipped with M60 Patton tanks. He placed the Qatari Brigade, supported by the 7th Battalion, 2d Saudi Arabian National Guard Brigade, in positions to block the road south from al-Khafji.[140]

Once established just south of the city, the Qatari Brigade began to engage targets of opportunity within the city. A platoon of Iraqi T-55 tanks emerged and engaged the Qatari AMX-30s, resulting in the destruction of three T-55s and the capture of a fourth. Iraqi prisoners revealed that there was close to an enemy "brigade in the city and another brigade was to join it."[141] In response, General Sultan bolstered the northern blocking force by committing the balance of the 8th Ministry of Defense and Aviation Brigade's armored battalion. The southern force was reinforced with the 8th Battalion, 2d Saudi Arabian National Guard, in addition to M113 armored personnel carriers equipped with antitank missile launchers from the 8th Ministry of Aviation and Defense Brigade.[142]

At 1152 on 30 January, 1st Battalion, 12th Marines, the Marine artillery battalion assigned to support the Saudi attack on al-Khafji, reported it had already expended 136 rounds of dual purpose improved conventional munitions and eight rounds of high explosive munitions.[143] The Cobra attack helicopters of Marine Light Attack Helicopter Squadron 367 continued to support the Marines along the frontier and in al-Khafji. For the same period, the squadron reported one tank, seven armored personnel carriers, one jeep, and one truck destroyed.[144]

At noon, Colonel Turki al-Firmi met with Colonel Admire. Colonel Turki was in command of the Saudi force specifically tasked with retaking al-Khafji. Captain Braden, the 1st ANGLICO officer assigned to Colonel Turki's brigade, observed the meeting. Colonel Admire told Colonel Turki that Marine reconnaissance teams were still in al-Khafji and briefed him on the 3d Marine plan to remove them from the city. Captain Braden recalled that "Col Turki stated that the city was his and that he had a tasking from 'Riyadh' to rescue the Marine Recon teams…. Col Turki asked if the Marines lacked trust in the Saudi abilities to perform their mission of defending their sector? The question of sector defense seemed moot at this point as the Iraqis were in control of al-Khafji, but the matter of trust between Coalition partners was in question."[145] Admire agreed and offered support.

Battery C, and later Battery A, 1st Battalion, 12th Marines, provided artillery fire, and a combined antiarmor team from 3d Marines moved to the gas station four kilometers south of al-Khafji.[146] Despite Saudi desires to fight the battle on their own, Marine air-naval gunfire liaison teams provided critical communications to the Saudis and coordinated artillery and air support. In addition, U.S. Army advisors from the Office of Program Manager for Modernization of the Saudi Arabian National Guard and civilian advisors from the Vinnell Corporation fought throughout the battle alongside their assigned Saudi units.

Colonel Admire said that acting as the supporting force was "one of the most difficult decisions I've ever had to make."[147] The decision to have the Saudis lead the attack to free al-Khafji shaped the rest of the battle. Marines would observe and aid their Coalition partners, but the Saudis and Qataris did the heavy fighting from this point on.[148]

As plans were being made to liberate al-Khafji, another strange event in the battle occurred. Two U.S. Army tractor-trailer heavy equipment transporters from the 233d Transportation Company drove into the city. The drivers were lost, unaware that they were in al-Khafji, and that an Iraqi offensive had occurred. One of the reconnaissance teams watched in horror as the two tractor-trailers drove into town, only to be met by a hail of fire from the Iraqis. The first of the two trucks was disabled and crashed, Iraqi fire having wounded its driver and assistant driver as well as disabling the steering. The second truck performed "the fastest U-turn in history, like he was a VW bug" and fled.[149] The Iraqis quickly overwhelmed and captured the two wounded soldiers, Specialist David Lockett and Specialist Melissa Rathbun-Nealy, whom were quickly transported back to Kuwait. Specialist Rathbun-Nealy was the first American female soldier captured since World War II. The two were not freed until after the war.[150]

Soon after the Army trucks disappeared into al-Khafji, Major Craig S. Huddleston was informed of their disappearance. On Colonel Admire's orders, 3d Battalion, 3d Marines, established an outpost, Check Point 67, south of the city to coordinate with the Saudis. Major Huddleston, the battalion's executive officer, was given command of the outpost.

The Saudi National Guard battalions, which freed al-Khafji from the Iraqis, employed Cadillac Gage V-150 Commando light armored vehicles, some of which were equipped with a M220 launcher for the BGM-71 TOW antitank missile.

DVIC DF-ST-91-04523

The Battle of al-Khafji

Photo courtesy of Capt Charles G. Grow
The water tower in southern al-Khafji was heavily damaged during the battle. It was a favorite target for both Iraqi and Saudi troops, and was strafed at least once by U.S. Marine Cobra helicopters.

He quickly formed a patrol to enter the town and recover the two soldiers; every one of the 128 Marines at the outpost volunteered to go, but he only took about 30 Marines. Huddleston mounted the patrol in humvees, including antitank missile and heavy machine gun vehicles, and headed for the city.[151]

Al-Khafji was still in a state of confusion. As the patrol raced into the town, they encountered some Iraqis but had no major fire fights. The Marines found the disabled tractor-trailer, but not the missing soldiers despite shouts of "U.S. Marines, U.S. Marines!" There was a short engagement with Iraqi armored personnel carriers, which Major Huddleston directed a pair of Cobras against. The patrol also found a destroyed Qatari AMX-30 tank and its dead crew. Disappointed, the Marines returned to the outpost. "We wanted to get them [the missing soldiers] pretty bad," Major Huddleston later said.[152]

Journalists, prevented by the prevailing press system and Saudi prohibitions against observing the battle in al-Khafji, began to congregate south of the town. Several spoke with Major Huddleston and others from the patrol, which led to a misunderstanding. The Coalition explained in press conferences that Saudi and Qatari forces were freeing al-Khafji, but the journalists who spoke with Major Huddleston mistook his brief patrol for a major Marine assault. They concluded that the Marines were doing the major fighting at al-Khafji, but that the Coalition was, for political reasons, giving credit for the battle to the Saudis. This myth was to persist; the belief that the military had lied to the press concerning al-Khafji would sour military-media relations long after the Gulf War ended.[153]

Meanwhile, General Khaled arrived at the Joint Forces Command-East headquarters south of al-Khafji. He was agitated, since King Fahd was pressuring him to liberate the city as quickly as possible. He also was upset about what he considered a lack of promised air from the Marine Corps. He contacted General Horner. "I told him I wanted air support as well as strikes by B-52s to break up Iraqi concentrations and prevent reinforcements reaching al-Khafji, even if it meant diverting air assets from the air campaign against strategic targets inside Iraq. Minimize raids on strategic targets and maximize them at al-Khafji, I urged him."[154]

General Horner saw the developing battle as an opportunity to inflict maximum losses on the Iraqis, but he did not consider the B-52 to be the proper weapon to use in this situation. He told General Khaled the same thing he routinely told ground commanders: "Don't tell me how to do the job. Tell me what you want done."[155]

Unsatisfied, General Khaled phoned Brigadier General Ahmad al-Sudairy, Saudi Director of Air Operations, an hour after he spoke to General Horner. "Forget about the Joint Forces. If the U.S. Air Force or the Marines don't come at once, I want you to take our air assets out of the Coalition and send them all to me! I need the Tornados, the F-5s, everything you've got!"[156] A few moments later the air assets General Horner had already designated for al-Khafji began to arrive. General Khaled was convinced his threat had worked and as General Boomer later said: "Ultimately, it was our air support that turned the tide for them."[157]

In addition to his distress over the lack of air, the two Marine teams in the city also presented General Khaled with a problem. "I was extremely worried that Schwartzkopf might use American troops, either U.S. Marines in an amphibious attack or a heliborne U.S. Army unit, to free *my* town in *my* sector. The shame would have been difficult to bear." Consequently, he ordered Major General Sultan's plan to talk the Iraqi's into surrendering be abandoned, and an immediate assault launched against the city.[158]

Given orders from General Khaled to attack at once, General Sultan passed the order to Colonel Turki, who in turn assigned the task of assaulting al-Khafji to Lieutenant Colonel Hamid Matar's 7th Battalion, 2d Saudi Arabian National Guard Brigade, supported by two Qatari tank companies.[159]

Captain Molofsky, the 3d Marines liaison officer, observed the Saudi preparations for battle. "Matar's Battalion is just really lined up on the road, you know – out into the desert a little bit, into Check Point 67. It's a beehive.... And, Matar's orders are to attack. And, that's it, you know—nothing else. Attack." Matar's battalion had received the order to attack at 1600, but it was not in position until 2000. Captain Molofsky observed that Matar was "really nervous; smoking cigarettes, pacing back and forth."[160]

There was a 15 minute preparatory fire by 1st Battalion, 12th Marines, and then the 7th Battalion literally charged forward against al-Khafji. "Out of nowhere, vehicles start up and people start driving forward," observed Captain Molofsky, who joined the 7th Battalion for the attack. The Saudi battalion drove straight up the middle of the road, but the Qatari tanks pulled to the side as the force approached al-Khafji. As the first couple Saudi vehicles entered under the arches of the city, "the whole place lights up," Molofsky said. "I mean a whole lot of directed fire, straight down the road ... just a firestorm of tracers, and tank main gun. And I notice a V-150 blow up, or it looked like it blew up, about 30 meters off to the side of the road."[161]

The Saudi attack was disorganized and undisciplined; they expended massive amounts of ammunition fired wildly into the city, as 1st ANGLICO reported afterwards. At one point, Qatari tanks fired on their Saudi allies although quick action by Captains Dillard and Gentil ended the fire before any casualties were taken. Still, the undisciplined fire and scattered assault was suspected to have caused two Saudi deaths.[162]

Lieutenant Colonel Michael Taylor was the U.S. Army advisor to the 7th Battalion and he aided Lieutenant Colonel Matar throughout the battle.[163] Throughout the night Saudi and Qatari soldiers fought against the Iraqi forces, suffering fire so heavy that Taylor, a Vietnam War veteran, described it as "flabbergasting."[164] But the Saudis and Qataris did not hesitate to return fire, as Captain Molofsky noted: "Qatari tanks came back up the road and were shooting up from behind and, at one point, the volume of fire got so heavy that we all got out of the truck and took cover in a ditch and you know the Saudis were shooting TOW missiles up in the air. Once they started shooting, they were shooting. I mean everybody was shooting at the max rate."[165]

Despite their efforts, the 7th Battalion was not able to retake al-Khafji nor was it able to relieve the reconnaissance teams still trapped within the city.[166] Captain Molofsky later recalled the engagement's surreal conclusion: "We pulled back into defilade in a small depression, just south of the city, and they [the Saudis] got out of the vehicles and they put their cloaks on, built fires and brewed up coffee, and then they prayed. I think my sense then was that the team couldn't have been much different than if they were riding with Lawrence except that they were mechanized vehicles instead of horses. Really extraordinary."[167]

North of al-Khafji

At nightfall, Lieutenant Colonel Naif's 5th Battalion, 2d Saudi Arabian National Guard Brigade, moved into position to block Iraqi movement in and out of al-Khafji from the north. The battalion was soon reinforced by a battalion of the 8th Ministry of Defense and Aviation Brigade, companies of which drifted north throughout the night. Iraqi forces attempted several times to reinforce al-Khafji, but Coalition air support was now available in copious amounts, and the air-naval gunfire teams attached to the 5th Battalion were able to call F/A-18s, AV-8s, and A-10s down on the Iraqi forces, inflicting a large number of casualties and forcing an even larger number of Iraqi troops to surrender to the Saudis.[168] The Saudis claimed 5 Iraqi vehicles destroyed, 6 captured, and 116 prisoners taken.[169]

The engagements were not without problems. The lack of joint training between the Saudi Arabian National Guard and Ministry of Defense and Aviation forces led the 8th Ministry of Defense and Aviation Battalion's commander to fear that the two Saudi forces might fire on each other, so in the morning he pulled back to refuel and rearm. This kept the Saudis from completely sealing al-Khafji at the end of the first night of battle, allowing a few Iraqi units to escape back into Kuwait.[170]

Coalition airpower was now focused on the al-Khafji area, taking advantage of the Iraqi offensive to strike at their forces which had previously remained hidden. The E-8C Joint Surveillance and Target Acquisition Radar System aircraft were used to track Iraqi movements in Kuwait. "The new JSTARS system proved a vital asset in beating back the Iraqi attacks," an Air Force study noted. "An airborne radar that could monitor enemy vehicle traffic at night with impressive clarity, JSTARS was an indispensable element in ensuring the efficient and effective use of Coalition aircraft."[171] The tactical air control center was focusing aircraft on al-Khafji and in-

Marines of 1st Battalion, 12th Marines, prepare an M198 155mm howitzer. The battalion fired numerous missions in support of Saudi and U.S. Marine forces during the Battle of al-Khafji.

History Division Photo

terdiction missions in southern Kuwait.

But the success of the air interdiction was not without loss. A U.S. Air Force AC-130, call sign "Spirit Zero Three," remained over its targets as the sun came up despite the policy that AC-130s only be employed at night. An Iraqi surface-to-air missile struck the aircraft, killing its 14-man crew.[172]

The massive effort had an effect on the Iraqi forces. General Salah Aboud had already begun requesting permission to withdraw. Although the offensive was termed "The Mother of Battles" by Saddam, General Salah radioed that "The mother was killing her children."[173]

31 January

Early in the morning on 31 January, Batteries A and C, 1st Battalion, 12th Marines, attached to the 3d Marines, fired an improved conventional munitions mission into al-Khafji under the control of the Marine reconnaissance teams inside the town.[174] Corporals Ingraham and Lentz, the team leaders, requested the artillery strike on a large Iraqi column between their positions at 0645. Initially, clearance was denied by 3d Marines fire support control center, but the mission was approved at 0701. At 0705, Batteries A and C responded to the call for fire. At 0740, 1st Battalion, 12th Marines, was told by the fire support control center that all future fire missions had to be approved by the air-naval gunfire teams attached to the Saudi forces.[175]

The barrage was a success from the perspective of the Marines inside al-Khafji, as it landed a solid blow against the Iraqis and essentially eliminated the Iraqi column. But it was placed dangerously close to their positions; Corporal Jeffrey Brown received a wound from the shrapnel.[176]

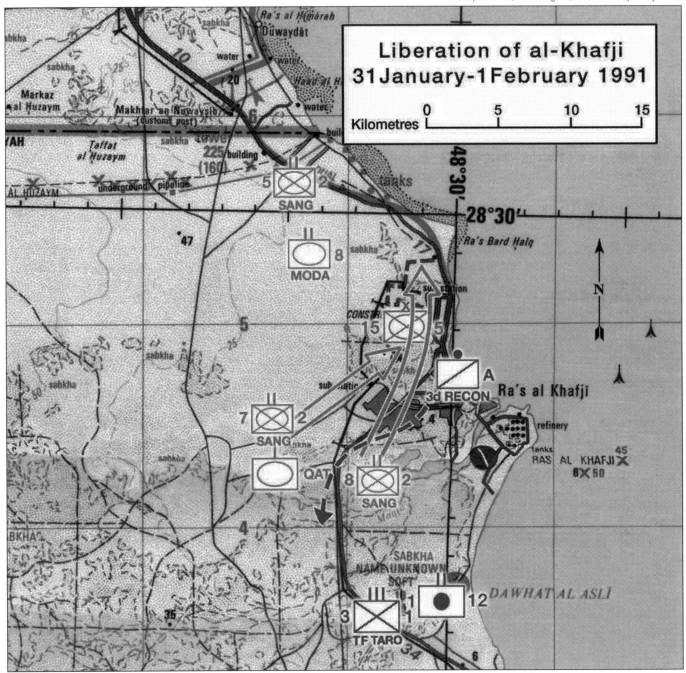

Ministry of Defense, United Kingdom, 1991, Modified by W. Stephen Hill

The fire came as a shock to the 1st ANGLICO teams maneuvering outside the city alongside the Saudis and Qataris, since Colonel Turki and Colonel Admire had agreed that all fire would be coordinated through the supporting arms liaison teams. Lieutenant Colonel William C. Grubb, Jr., 1st ANGLICO commander, went to the 3d Marines combat operations center and fixed the fire support coordination problem, which led to the order that all fire missions be approved by the air-naval gunfire teams. Despite these attempts to avoid firing on Coalition forces, the Qatari's claimed one of their AMX-30s was disabled by Marine artillery fire, although it was not confirmed.[177]

Meanwhile, the 7th Battalion, 2d Saudi Arabian National Guard Brigade, was preparing another attempt to storm al-Khafji and relieve the reconnaissance teams. This time, the attack was more carefully prepared, with artillery support from both Saudi and Marine artillery units and extensive Marine close air support coordinated by the teams working alongside the Saudi Arabian National Guard units. Despite the air and artillery support, the Iraqis still put up a fierce fight, destroying three Saudi V-150 armored cars.[178] "Tank main gun, recoilless rifle, TOW [antitank missile], and small arms fire came thick and furious," 1st ANGLICO later reported. "The Saudis and Qataris charged through the streets firing at everything and anything and in every direction."[179]

The battle raged through the southern half of al-Khafji, while Marine AV-8B Harriers and AH-1W Cobras provided direct support to the Saudi and Qatari troops. Air-naval gunfire teams directed the Cobras in a strafing run against the town's water tower, and Harriers destroyed Iraqi vehicles at the major road intersection in that quarter of the city.[180] The Marine reconnaissance teams took advantage of the confusion of this assault to withdraw safely from al-Khafji, one on foot, the other team in humvees that had sat inside a courtyard, undetected by the Iraqis since the first hours of the battle.[181]

In the afternoon, the 7th Battalion withdrew to rest and resupply, and the 8th Battalion, 2d Saudi Arabian National Guard Brigade, took its place clearing al-Khafji buildings. By this point the Saudis had lost 7 Cadillac Gage V-150 Armored Cars, 18 dead, and 50 wounded. The clearing operation continued throughout the night. "Saudi urban operations were different than what Americans practice," Captain Braden later noted. "Instead of room-by-room clearing, they simply occupy a block and if they take fire they target with TOWs and heavy machine guns until resistance stops and then move to the next building of street. As a result of these techniques there were numerous pockets of Iraqis left in the city that would be killed or captured over the next few days."[182]

In the north, 5th Battalion, 2d Saudi National Guard, and its attached air-naval gunfire teams under Captain Kleinsmith and First Lieutenant Paul B. Deckert stopped Iraqi units trying to reinforce their forces in al-Khafji. At Observation Post 7, a battery of Iraqi self-propelled howitzers had taken up position, supported by infantry and armored personnel carriers. A division of four Cobras destroyed the battery under Captain Kleinsmith's direction, but their arrival coincided with the destruction by enemy fire of two Saudi armored cars and an ambulance. Convinced that they had suffered friendly fire, the Saudis withdrew, leaving Captain Kleinsmith and his team to stabilize the line with air support. When the immediate Iraqi threats were removed, Kleinsmith's team rejoined the 5th Battalion.[183]

As the ground fight for al-Khafji drew to a close, the air effort continued to devastate the Iraqi forces. After a slow start, Coalition air forces claimed hundreds of tanks, armored personnel carriers, and artillery tubes destroyed during the five

Operating in their doctrinal role as part of the Marine air-ground task force, AV-8B Harriers provided needed close air support during the Battle of al-Khafji.

History Division Photo

The Battle of al-Khafji

days that al-Khafji remained the main effort. An Air Force post war study highlighted the effect of the air attacks: "pilots described the frantic maneuverings of surviving Iraqi vehicles as visually equivalent to the results of 'turning on the light in a cockroach-infested apartment.'" The report added: "perhaps the most revealing comment of all came from a member of the Iraqi *5th Mechanized Division* who had fought in the Iran-Iraq War. This veteran soldier stated that Coalition airpower imposed more damage on his brigade in half an hour than it had sustained in eight years of fighting against the Iranians."[184]

The next morning, 1 February, Saudi units advanced all the way through al-Khafji, encountering only light resistance. They cleared the city of remaining Iraqi troops, although solitary holdouts would appear to surrender over the next few days, and established a defensive position north of the city. The Battle of al-Khafji had ended.[185]

Considerations

Every battle has losses. During the Battle of al-Khafji, 25 Americans lost their lives, 11 Marines and 14 airmen. Three Marines were wounded and two soldiers captured by the enemy. One LAV-25, one LAV-AT, and one AC-130 gunship were destroyed. The Saudis and Qataris suffered 18 killed and 50 wounded. Ten armored cars and two tanks were destroyed. After the war, the Iraqis claimed to have destroyed 4 helicopters, 30 tanks, and 58 armored personnel carriers, as well as capturing 13 prisoners.[186] They listed their losses as 71 dead, 148 wounded, and 702 missing, as well as 186 vehicles destroyed, but their actual losses were likely higher. In the immediate vicinity of al-Khafji alone, 1st ANGLICO reported 90 vehicles destroyed, at least 300 Iraqi soldiers killed, and 680 captured. By most accounts, the *6th Brigade, 3d Armored Division* was badly mauled and the *15th, 20th,* and *26th Brigades* of the *5th Mechanized Division* were nearly destroyed.[187]

The Battle of al-Khafji had some immediate consequences. The deaths which occurred in the early morning hours of 30 January, when an Air Force A-10 fired the missile into the Marine LAV-25, were one of several similar events during January. As a result, General Boomer ordered an investigation to determine what measures could be taken to prevent future casualties. The investigation team's report was completed prior to the invasion of Kuwait and its recommendations implemented.

Otherwise, Marines, Saudis, and Iraqis all took differing views of the battle. Marines generally took away an increased confidence in techniques and doctrines, and a clearer idea of the enemy they would face. Lieutenant Colonel Myers felt that the screening forces along the border had exceeded expectations and the battle "proved the concept, philosophically" of the light armored vehicle.[188] Captain Braden saw al-Khafji as proof of the value and importance of the air-naval gunfire liaison company, and long after the battle ended, he was using al-Khafji as an example to argue against its disbandment: "Without ANGLICO, it is difficult to envision another successful Battle of al-Khafji," he wrote.[189]

Marines gained confidence in their Saudi allies. Colonel Admire, for one, now felt there was "no doubt in the Marine Corps force's mind that when the time would come to in fact attack into Kuwait, the Saudis and the Qataries and the Coalition forces would be with us. Absolutely no doubt."[190] Captain Molofsky agreed because "when push came to shove, without any real plan, any real direction, those Saudi soldiers obeyed their orders and went forward. And, they did so courageously."[191]

General Boomer saw al-Khafji as further proof that the Iraqi military was a hollow force. "We knew they weren't motivated even by the time al-Khafji occurred, and it confirmed it. We were beginning to pick up POWs who said, 'I don't want any part of this deal. I am down here getting the heck pounded out of me everyday, food and water are short. Why am I here?' In essence they were saying, 'I don't want to die here, in this conflict.' We were getting enough of that so that I really came to believe that there was a significant morale problem on the other side."[192] But for Captain Molofsky, the view at the tactical level was somewhat different: "My opinion was that; if that's what it was gonna take to get started in the recovery of a small town like al-Khafji, that we were gonna be involved in

Photo courtesy of Cpl Charles H. Ingraham III

Cpl Jeffery D. Brown of 3d Platoon, Company A, 3d Reconnaissance Battalion, stands in one of his team's humvees. The humvee's tires were punctured and its windshield shattered by shrapnel from a Marine artillery barrage called in on Iraqi forces near the reconnaissance teams' positions. Cpl Brown was wounded by the same artillery strike.

Marine Corps Art Collection

Marines of 3d Battalion, 3d Marines, search al-Khafji for Iraqi stragglers and examine the battle damage as depicted in the painting "Cleaning up Khafji" by Capt Charles G. Grow.

a prolonged and bloody struggle."[193]

The U.S. Air Force saw the Battle of al-Khafji as the proof of air power: "The Battle of Khafji was preeminently an airpower victory." Close air support and battlefield interdiction had isolated the battlefield and inflicted great destruction upon the Iraqis. The result was a "devastating defeat" for the Iraqi military and "airpower was the decisive element."[194]

General Khaled bin Sultan explained that while the battle was such an important victory for the Saudis had it gone badly, "the blow to our morale would have been severe. But victory changed the mood of our soldiers to an amazing degree. They had been given a chance to prove themselves and had done so splendidly.... Our forces were now equal partners with our allies, ready to play a full role in any future battle."[195]

Perhaps the most surprising conclusion concerning the Battle of al-Khafji came from the Iraqis. Iraqi post-war studies present al-Khafji as a victory whose techniques and procedures should be emulated to ensure future success. The Iraqis were able to plan and launch a major offensive despite the Coalition's air power advantage. They succeeded in capturing al-Khafji and held it for two days against an enemy superior in technology and numbers.[196] As General Salah Aboud concluded: "The al-Khafji conflict is on the list of the bright conflicts in Iraqi Army history.... one of the thousands recorded in the Iraqi Army history for the new generations."[197]

In the end everyone but the dead and wounded won the Battle of al-Khafji. Although the battle did not accomplish any of the Iraqi objectives, it presented enough of an appearance of success that Saddam was able to claim a credible propaganda victory. After the war, the Iraqis were convinced that the battle had somehow influenced the Coalition's decision to end the war after evicting the Iraqis from Kuwait, but before removing Saddam Hussein from power.

The Saudis faced an invasion of their territory and defeated it. Although Coalition air power undoubtedly played a key role in the defeat of the Iraqi offensive, it was the bravery of the Saudi ground troops, with American advisors, who actually ejected the Iraqis from Saudi soil. Al-Khafji has entered Saudi military history as a great victory.

For the Americans, al-Khafji was won almost by accident. American forces proved so superior that it did not completely register that a major Iraqi offensive had occurred. As a result, U.S. Central Command planners did not expect the Iraqis to collapse as quickly as they did in the February invasion.[198]

At al-Khafji, all of the Marine deaths were caused by U.S. fire, but that should not detract from their sacrifice, nor from the bravery of the Marines who survived the battle through luck and training. Endorsing the final report on the Marines killed by the A-10's missile, General Boomer said: "The technological marvels that helped the Coalition forces defeat Iraq sometimes fail, and with disastrous results.... Marines, heroes in my heart, lost their lives while repelling an enemy force. They were good Marines."[199]

The Battle of al-Khafji

Al-Khafji Order of Battle

U.S. Marine Forces

I Marine Expeditionary Force — Lieutenant General Walter E. Boomer

    1st Surveillance, Reconnaissance, and Intelligence Group — Colonel Michael V. Brock
    1st Air Naval Gunfire Liaison Company — Lieutenant Colonel William C. Grubb, Jr.

1st Marine Division — Major General James M. Myatt

    1st Reconnaissance Battalion — Lieutenant Colonel Michael L. Rapp
    1st Light Armored Infantry Battalion (Task Force Shepherd) — Lieutenant Colonel Clifford O. Myers III
    1st Battalion, 12th Marines — Lieutenant Colonel Robert W. Rivers
    3d Marines — Colonel John H. Admire

2d Marine Division — Major General William M. Keys

    2d Light Armored Infantry Battalion — Lieutenant Colonel Keith T. Holcomb

3d Marine Aircraft Wing — Major General Royal N. Moore, Jr.

    Marine Light Attack Helicopter Squadron 367 — Lieutenant Colonel Terry J. Frerker
    Marine Light Attack Helicopter Squadron 369 — Lieutenant Colonel Michael M. Kurth

Saudi Arabian and Qatari Forces

Joint Forces Command — General Khaled bin Sultan bin Saud

Joint Forces Command East — Major General Sultan 'Adi al-Mutairi

2d Saudi Arabian National Guard Brigade — Colonel Turki Abdulmohsin al-Firmi

    5th Battalion, 2d Saudi Arabian National Guard Brigade — Lieutenant Colonel Naif
    7th Battalion, 2d Saudi Arabian National Guard Brigade — Lieutenant Colonel Hamid Matar
    8th Battalion, 2d Saudi Arabian National Guard Brigade — Lieutenant Colonel Hamud

Qatari Brigade — Lieutenant Colonel Ali Saeed

Iraqi Forces

III Corps — Major General Salah Aboud Mahmoud

5th Mechanized Division — Brigadier General Flyeh Yaseen

    15th Mechanized Brigade — Colonel Khalif Hamid
    26th Mechanized Brigade — Colonel Amid Abduljabir
    20th Mechanized Brigade — —

3d Armored Division — Brigadier General Hussan Zedin

    6th Armored Brigade — Colonel Ibdil Raziq Mahmoud

IV Corps — Major General Yaiyd Khalel Zaki

1st Mechanized Division — Brigadier General Hussen

Notes

[1] This section based on material from LtCol James R. Braden, "The Battle of Khafji: A Coalition Air Ground Task Force Victory" (Paper, USMC Command and Staff College, 1999), p. 11-12, hereafter Braden, "Khafji"; see also Williamson Murray, *Air War in the Persian Gulf* (Baltimore: Nautical & Aviation Publishing Company, 1995), hereafter Murray, *Air War in the Persian Gulf*; Lieutenant General Bernard E. Trainor and Michael R. Gordon, *The Generals' War* (Boston: Little, Brown and Company, 1995), hereafter Gordon and Trainor, *Generals' War*.

[2] James Titus, "The Battle of Khafji: An Overview and Preliminary Analysis" (Paper, Air University, 1996), p. 7, hereafter Titus, "Khafji."

[3] Northrop Grumman Corp., "Joint Stars Data Analysis: The Battle of Khafji" (Paper, USAF Studies and Analysis Agency, 1997), p. 18.

[4] This section based on material from Kevin M. Woods, et al., *Iraqi Perspectives Project: A View of Operation Iraqi Freedom from Saddam's Senior Leadership* (Joint Center for Operational Analysis, u.d.), hereafter *Iraqi Perspectives*; Captured Iraqi War College Study, Al-Khafji Conflict (ISGQ-2003-00046031), hereafter Iraqi War College Study; Kenneth M. Pollack, *Arabs at War: Military Effectiveness 1948-1991* (London: University of Nebraska Press, 2002), hereafter Pollack, *Arabs at War*.

[5] *Iraqi Perspectives*, p. 6.

[6] Ibid., pp. 15, 20.

[7] Ibid., p. 16.

[8] Ibid., p. 95.

[9] Ibid.

[10] Ibid.

[11] Ibid.

[12] Ibid., p. 96.

[13] Edgar O'Ballance, *The Gulf War* (New York; Brassey's Defense Publishers, 1988), summary of discussion on pp. 94, 143-145, 164-166, 173-174, 194; Gordon and Trainor, *Generals' War*, p. 268-269; LtCol Peter J. Palmer, "Battle of Khafji: A Gulf State Perspective" (Paper, Marine Corps University, u.d.), hereafter Palmer, "Gulf State."

[14] *How They Fight: Desert Shield Order of Battle Handbook*, AIA-DS-2-90 (1990); DOD, *Iraq Country Handbook*, DOD-2600-642794, (1994).

[15] Iraqi War College Study; Captured Iraqi Training Pamphlet, Battle of al-Khafji (ISGQ-2003-00054592), hereafter Iraqi Training Pamphlet.

[16] Iraqi War College Study, pp. 104-105.

[17] Air War College Study, "EPW Interviews" (Maxwell AFB: Air Force Historical Research Agency); Palmer, "Gulf State."

[18] Iraqi War College Study, p. 101.

[19] Bruce R. Nardulli, "Dance of Swords: U.S. Military Assistance to Saudi Arabia, 1942-1964" (unpublished Phd Dissertation, The Ohio State University, 2002).

[20] Mohamed Heikal, *Illusions of Triumph* (New York: HarperCollins, 1992).

[21] Anthony H. Cordesman, *Saudi Arabia*, (Boulder: Westview Press, 1997), p. 122, hereafter Cordesman, *Saudi Arabia*; Palmer, "Gulf State."

[22] Cordesman, *Saudi Arabia*, p. 137; Palmer, "Gulf State"; Martin Stanton, *Road to Baghdad* (New York, Ballantine Books, 2003), hereafter Stanton, *Road to Baghdad*.

[23] Stanton, *Road to Baghdad,* pp. 14-18; Braden, "Khafji," pp. 5, 23, 29-30; Palmer, "Gulf State."

[24] General Khaled bin Sultan, *Desert Warrior* (New York:, Harper & Collins Publishers, 1995), hereafter Khaled, *Desert Warrior*.

[25] Ibid., p. 379.

[26] Col Joseph Molofsky intvw with author, 30Jun06 and 16Aug06 (MCHC, Quantico, VA), hereafter Molofsky intvw, 30Jun06 or Molofsky intvw, 16Aug06.

[27] Stanton, *Road to Baghdad*, pp. 23-25.

[28] LtCol D. P. Hughes, "Battle for Khafji: 29Jan/1 Feb 1991," *Defense Quarterly*, pp. 15-22; Palmer, "Gulf State."

[29] BGen Thomas V. Draude intvw with author and Dr. Fred Allison, 21Jun06 (MCHC, Quantico, VA).

[30] Col John A. Admire intvw, CD 10234 (Grey Research Center, Quantico, VA), hereafter Admire intvw.

[31] Molofsky intvw, 30Jun06, 16Aug06; Braden, "Khafji," p. 8

[32] Molofsky intvw, 16Aug06.

[33] Braden, "Khafji," pp. 8-9.

[34] Ibid., pp. 6-7.

[35] Titus, "Khafji," p. 9; Gordon and Trainor, *Generals' War*, pp. 268-269.

[36] Molofsky intvw, 16Aug06.

[37] 1st Air-Naval Gunfire Liaison Company/1st Surveillance, Reconnaisance, Intelligence Group After Action Report for the Battle of Khafji, 29Jan91-1Feb91(MCHC, Quantico VA), hereafter ANGLICO AAR.

[38] LtCol Clifford O. Myers intvw by LtCol Charles H. Cureton, 8Mar91 (MCHC, Quantico, VA), hereafter Myers intvw, 8Mar91.

[39] Khaled, *Desert Warrior*; Braden, pp. 7-8; Palmer, "Gulf State."

[40] Maj Steven M. Zimmeck, *U.S. Marines in the Persian Gulf, 1990-1991: Combat Service Support in Desert Shield and Desert Storm.* (Washington, D.C.: History and Museums Division, Headquarters, U.S. Marine Corps, 1999), p. 108.

[41] Molofsky intvw, 16Aug06.

[42] Braden, "Khafji," p. 8.

[43] Leroy D. Stearns, *U.S. Marines in the Persian Gulf, 1990-1991: With the 3d Marine Aircraft Wing in Desert Shield and Desert Storm* (Washington, D.C.: History and Museums Division, Headquarters, U.S. Marine Corps, 1999), p.122; LtCol Charles H. Cureton, *U.S. Marines in the Persian Gulf, 1990-1991: With the 1st Marine Division in Desert Shield and Desert Storm* (Washington, D.C.: History and Museums Division, Headquarters, U.S. Marine Corps, 1993), pp. 26-28.

[44] Iraqi War College Study, p. 97.

[45] Ibid., pp. 99-101.

[46] Ibid., p. 98.

[47] Ibid., p. 99.

[48] Ibid., p. 103.

[49] Gordon and Trainor, *Generals' War*, p. 269.

[50] Iraqi War College Study, pp. 104-107.

[51] Titus, "Khafji," p. 7.

[52] Braden, "Khafji," p. 13.

[53] Ibid.

[54] Ibid.

[55] Ibid., pp. 13-14.

[56] ANGLICO AAR.

[57] Braden, "Khafji," pp. 13-14.

[58] David J. Morris, *Storm on the Horizon* (New York: Free Press, 2004), p. 145, hereafter Morris, *Storm*.

[59] Iraqi War College Study.

[60] Morris, *Storm*, p. 145.

[61] Iraqi War College Study, pp. 108-109.

[62] Ibid., pp. 144-146.

[63] Ibid., pp. 108-109.

[64] Braden, "Khafji," p. 14.

[65] ANGLICO AAR.

[66] Braden, "Khafji," p. 14.

[67] Morris, *Storm*, pp. 31-32.

[68] Ibid., Ch. 1.

[69] Ibid., pp. 3, 31-34.

[70] Morris, *Storm* p. 50; Roger Pollard, "The Battle for Op-4: Start of the Ground War," *Marine Corps Gazette*, Mar92, hereafter Pollard, "Op-4"; Myers intvw, 8Mar91; 1st LAI ComdC, Jan-Feb91 (Gray Research Center, Quantico, VA).

[71] Pollard, "Op-4"; Myers intvw, 8Mar91; 1st LAI ComdC, Jan-Feb91 (Gray Research Center, Quantico, VA).

[72] Iraqi War College Study, pp. 120-125.

[73] Morris, *Storm*, pp. 1-6.

[74] Pollard, "Op-4"; Myers intvw, 8Mar91.

[75] Morris, *Storm*, pp. 66-73.

[76] Pollard, "Op-4."

[77] Ibid.

[78] Lt David Kendall intvw, 7Feb91 (Gray Research Center, Quantico, VA).

[79] Pollard, "Op-4."

[80] Pollard, "Op-4"; Pollard, Capt Roger L. intvw with LtCol Charles H. Cureton, CD# 10441 (Gray Research Center, Quantico, VA), hereafter Pollard, intvw.

[81] Lt David Kendall intvw, 7Feb91 (Gray Research Center, Quantico, VA).

[82] Pollard, "Op-4"; 1st LAI ComdC, Jan-Feb91 (Gray Research Center, Quantico, VA).

[83] Fratricide - Investigation into USAF At-

tack on Marine LAV, SWA-0062, Seq. No. 01980 (MCLLS, Quantico, VA)

[84] Pollard intvw.

[85] Ibid.

[86] Myers intvw, 8Mar91.

[87] Pollard, "Op-4"; Pollard intvw; Myers intvw, 8Mar91.

[88] Iraqi War College Study, pp. 120-125.

[89] Ibid., pp. 144-146.

[90] Ibid., pp. 120-125.

[91] 2d LAI ComdC, Jan-Feb91 (Gray Research Center, Quantico, VA).

[92] Ibid.

[93] Ibid.

[94] Titus, "Khafji," p. 12; Dennis P. Mroczkowski, *U.S. Marines in the Persian Gulf, 1990-1991: With the 2d Marine Division in Desert Shield and Desert Storm* (Washington: HQMC, 1993), pp. 20-23; Gordon and Trainor, *Generals' War*, pp. 274-275.

[95] Morris, *Storm*, pp. 114-118.

[96] Titus, "Khafji," p. 12; Gordon and Trainor, *Generals' War*, p. 275; Morris, *Storm*, pp. 119-125.

[97] Titus, "Khafji," p. 12.

[98] Pollard, "Op-4"; 1st LAI ComdC, Jan-Feb91 (Gray Research Center, Quantico, VA).

[99] ANGLICO AAR; Braden, "Khafji," p. 15.

[100] ANGLICO AAR.

[101] Ibid.

[102] Braden, "Khafji," p. 14.

[103] ANGLICO AAR.

[104] Khaled, *Desert Warrior*, p. 366.

[105] Palmer, "Gulf State."

[106] Titus, "Khafji," p. 13; Gordon and Trainor, *Generals' War*, pp. 279-286; Khaled, *Desert Warrior*, pp. 381-387; Rick Atkinson, *Crusade: The Untold Story of the Persian Gulf War* (Boston: Houghton Mifflin, 1993), pp. 208-213, hereafter Atkinson, *Crusade.*

[107] Braden, "Khafji," p. 14.

[108] ANGLICO AAR.

[109] Molofsky intvw, 16Aug06.

[110] Khaled, *Desert Warrior*, p. 368.

[111] Ibid., p. 365.

[112] Ibid., p. 368.

[113] Braden, "Khafji," p. 15.

[114] Titus, "Khafji," p. 11.

[115] Titus, "Khafji," p. 11; Gordon and Trainor, *Generals' War*, pp. 273, 278.

[116] HMLA-367 ComdC, Jan91, and HMLA-369 ComdC, Jan91 (Gray Research Center, Quantico, VA).

[117] Leroy D. Stearns, *U.S. Marines in the Persian Gulf, 1990-1991: With the 3d Marine Aircraft Wing in Desert Shield and Desert Storm* (Washington, D.C.: History and Museums Division, Headquarters, U.S. Marine Corps, 1999), pp. 124-125.

[118] Morris, *Storm*, p. 150-158.

[119] Clifton A Barnes, "In Every Clime and Place," *Leatherneck*, Aug91, pp. 16-20.

[120] Titus, "Khafji," p. 10; Friedman, pp.197-198; 160; Gordon and Trainor, *Generals' War*, pp. 268-269; *Shield and Sword*, p. 227-229.

[121] ANGLICO AAR; Braden, "Khafji," p. 15.

[122] Ibid.

[123] Ibid.

[124] Ibid.

[125] Iraqi War College Study, p. 111.

[126] Ibid., pp. 120-125.

[127] Ibid., pp. 147-148.

[128] Ibid., pp. 125-126.

[129] Morris, *Storm*, pp. 166-169.

[130] 1st Recon ComdC, Jan-Mar91 and 3d Recon ComdC, Jan-Feb91, (Gray Research Center, Quantico, VA).

[131] Molofsky intvw, 30Jun06.

[132] Morris, *Storm*, pp. 159-166.

[133] I Marine Expeditionary Force Commander's Morning Briefing, 30Jan91.

[134] Boomer intvw 27Jul06.

[135] Khaled, *Desert Warrior*, p. 364.

[136] Ibid., p. 376.

[137] ANGLICO AAR.

[138] Ibid.

[139] Ibid.

[140] Braden, "Khafji," p. 16.

[141] ANGLICO AAR.

[142] ANGLICO AAR; Braden, "Khafji," pp. 16-17.

[143] ANGLICO AAR.

[144] 1/12 ComdC, Jan-Feb91 (Gray Research Center, Quantico, VA).

[145] HMLA-367 ComdC, Jan91 (Gray Research Center, Quantico, VA).

[146] Braden, "Khafji," pp. 19-20.

[147] Ibid.

[148] Admire intvw.

[149] Ibid.

[150] Morris, *Storm*, pp. 194.

[151] Ibid., pp. 193-196.

[152] Ibid., pp. 196-197.

[153] R. R. Keene, "In Every Clime and Place," *Leatherneck*, Mar91, pp. 22-27; Morris, *Storm*, pp. 196-198; Otto Lehrack, *America's Battalion* (Tuscaloosa: University of Alabama Press, 2005), pp. 128-131.

[154] David H. Mould, "Press Pools and Military-Media Relations in the Gulf War: A Case Study of the Battle of Khafji, January 1991," *Historical Journal of Film, Radio & Television*, Jun96, p. 133.

[155] Khaled, *Desert Warrior*, p. 374.

[156] Gordon and Trainor, *Generals' War*, p.279.

[157] Khaled, *Desert Warrior*, p. 374.

[158] Boomer intvw, 27Jul06.

[159] Khaled, *Desert Warrior*, p. 378.

[160] Braden, "Khafji," p. 20; Khaled, *Desert Warrior*; pp. 362-390. LtCol Martin N. Stanton, "The Saudi Arabian National Guard Motorized Brigades," *Armor*, Mar-Apr96, pp. 6-11.

[161] Molofsky intvw, 16Aug06.

[162] Ibid.

[163] ANGLICO AAR.

[164] Stanton, *Road to Baghdad*, p. 261.

[165] Ibid., p. 262.

[166] Molofsky intvw, 16Aug06.

[167] Stanton, *Road to Baghdad*, pp. 262-264; Braden, "Khafji," pp. 20-22.

[168] Molofsky intvw, 30Jun06.

[169] Braden, "Khafji," pp. 22-23.

[170] Stanton, *Road to Baghdad*, p. 266.

[171] Palmer, "Gulf State."

[172] Titus, "Khafji," pp. 13-14.

[173] Titus, "Khafji," pp. 17-20; Gordon and Trainor, *Generals' War*, p. 284. The most detailed secondary account of the shoot down is in Rick Atkinson, *Crusade: The Untold Story of the Gulf War* (Boston: Houghton Mifflin, 1993), p. 210.

[174] Gordon and Trainor, *Generals' War*, pp. 283, 285-287.

[175] Morris, *Storm,* p. 253; ANGLICO AAR.

[176] 1/12 ComdC, Jan-Feb91 (Gray Research Center, Quantico, VA).

[177] Morris, *Storm*, pp. 253-258.

[178] ANGLICO AAR; Braden, "Khafji," p. 17.

[179] Braden, "Khafji," pp. 22-23.

[180] ANGLICO AAR.

[181] Ibid.

[182] Morris, *Storm*, pp. 258-266.

[183] Braden, "Khafji," p. 23-24.

[184] ANGLICO AAR.

[185] Titus, "Khafji," pp. 17-20; General Mahmoud's comments and the references to Iraqi radio communications are taken from Gordon and Trainor, *Generals' War*, pp. 283, 285-87; the "cockroach" analogy appears in H. Norman Schwarzkopf, *It Doesn't Take a Hero* (New York: Linda Grey, Bantam, 1992), p. 429.

[186] ANGLICO AAR.

[187] Iraqi Training Pamphlet.

[188] ANGLICO AAR.

[189] Myers intvw, 8Mar91.

[190] Braden, "Khafji," p. 32.

[191] Admire intvw.

[192] Molofsky intvw, 30Jun06.

[193] Boomer intvw, 27Jul06 (MCHC, Quantico, VA).

[194] Molofsky intvw, 16Aug06.

[195] Titus, "Khafji"; Barry D. Watts, et al., "Effects and Effectiveness," *The Gulf War Air Power Survey* Volume II, Eliot A. Cohen, et al. 6 vols. (Washington, D.C.: Government Printing Office, 1993), p. 240.

[196] Khaled, *Desert Warrior*, p. 390.

[197] Iraqi War College Study, p. 97.

[198] Ibid.

[199] Gordon and Trainor, *Generals' War*, p. 288.

[200] Fratricide - Investigation into USAF Attack on Marine LAV, SWA-0062, Seq. No. 01980 (MCLLS, Quantico, VA).

About the Author
And Acknowledgements

Paul W. Westermeyer received a Master of Arts degree in history from the Ohio State University in 1996, and is pursuing a doctorate in history from the same institution. He joined the staff of the History Division in 2005. The Iraqi documents used as sources for this project were translated by Ali al Saadee; the project could not have been completed without his excellent work. The finished manuscript also benefited from the aid and advice of David J. Morris, Dr. Kevin Osterloh, and Dr. Amin Tarzi. History Division interns Alexander N. Hinman, Nicholas J. Ross, Evan Sills, and Paul R. Zimmerman provided invaluable research assistance.

This work could not have been published without the professional efforts of the staff of the History Division. Dr. Nathan S. Lowrey provided invaluable professional advice and support. The author would like to thank Charles D. Melson, Charles R. Smith, Greg Macheak, and Major Valerie A. Jackson for their comments and revisions. W. Stephen Hill designed and produced the layout, including maps. Peggy F. Frierson prepared the art and photographs for this publication.

History Division
United States Marine Corps
Washington, D.C.
2008
PCN 106 000 400

Background Photo: For wounds suffered during the Battle of al-Khafji, Cpl Jeffery D. Brown of 3d Platoon, Company A, 3d Reconnaissance Battalion, receives the Purple Heart at Manifa Bay, Saudi Arabia, following the war.
Photo courtesy of Cpl Charles H. Ingraham III

Back Cover: The logotype reproduced on the back cover has as its major element the oldest military insignia in continuous use in the United States. It first appeared, as shown here, on Marine Corps buttons adopted in 1804. With the stars changed to five points, the device has continued on Marine Corps buttons to the present day.

Made in the USA
Monee, IL
16 February 2024

53634251R00024